A Record in Detail

A Record in Detail

The Architectural Photographs of Jack E. Boucher

With an Introduction
by
William H. Pierson, Jr.

University of Missouri Press
Columbia, 1988

Copyright © 1988 by
The Curators of the University of Missouri
University of Missouri Press, Columbia,
Missouri 65211
Printed and bound in Japan

Library of Congress Cataloging-in-Publication Data

Boucher, Jack E.

A record in detail: Architectural photographs of
Jack E. Boucher

Book to accompany the traveling exhibition of
Boucher's photographs mounted by the Historic
American Buildings Survey and the Library of Con-
gress.   1. Photography, Architectural—United
States—Exhibitions. 2. Boucher, Jack E.—Exhibitions.
3. Historic buildings—United States—Pictorial
works—Exhibitions.   I. Historic American Buildings
Survey.   II. Library of Congress.   III. Title.
TR659.B676   1987   779'.4'0924 87–5828
ISBN 0-8262-0640-9 (alk. paper)

Photograph this page: David Ogden house, view of
staircase as seen from the front door.

Acknowledgments

A quarter-century of architectural photography for HABS could not have passed without my having accumulated an enormous debt of gratitude to many people. This book, and the exhibit it reflects, are the result of my humble effort to document structures for posterity.

None of this would have come to pass had it not been for the interest and efforts of Robert J. Kapsch, Chief of the National Park Service's HABS/HAER Division and my boss. Book, exhibit, and more were his concept, and I am most appreciative.

Selecting 145 photographs from the 55,000 I've taken over the years for the exhibit was the incredible chore of my colleague and friend Bill Lebovich, a fine architectural historian for HABS/HAER and an enthusiastic photographer in his own right. He subsequently boiled the 145 views down to 74 illustrations for this book, no mean task itself. I can never repay him for the hundred of hours of effort he expended on my behalf.

I'm grateful to the distinguished architectural historian Bill Pierson for his enormous contribution to this volume, an essay that must be a first of its kind, a study of the role of architectural photography in architectural scholarship and documentation.

There are others no less important. William Miner, Exhibits Officer of the Library of Congress, lavished his considerable talent to design the exhibit, and he was helped by his right-hand man Tom Beecher, Traveling Exhibits Specialist, and other colleagues. My hat is off to Dan Gross, Photo Lab Chief for CESI Inc. of Rockville, Maryland, who holds the contract to provide our laboratory services, and his very capable lab technician and printer Valerie Nyce. It was Valerie who made the 11 x 14 enlargements for reproduction in this book.

Readers, who scrutinize and criticize a manuscript, seldom receive recognition and sometimes, depending on their comments, prefer it that way. A very good friend of long standing, Jim Massey, former Chief of HABS/HAER, served as a reader for this volume, and I am indebted to him for his thoughtful and objective comments.

The American Institute of Architects has enthusiastically supported the Historic American Buildings Survey since the beginning of the program in 1933 when it co-signed the tripartite agreement creating HABS. I am deeply grateful to them. I received their annual medal for architectural photography in 1981; in the case of the present exhibit, they made available the foyer of the AIA National Headquarters for the opening and produced a superb poster. Special thanks to Bruce M. Kriviskey, AIA/AICP, the Director of Urban Design and Historic Preservation Programs; to John Hoke, Publisher, AIA Press; to Allen Freeman, Managing Editor of *Architecture Magazine;* and to Ann Parenteau, Senior Manager of Marketing.

Work over the years has been pleasant and rewarding because of my colleagues, the extraordinary staff of the HABS/HAER Division, a dedicated group of professionals who are a credit to the Federal Service.

Finally, and most important, my wife Peggy and sons Jack and Paul deserve my love and thanks, not only for their support in the usual family ways, but because all three have given unselfishly of their time and energy to physically work with me, both in the field and in the lab, contributing thousands of hours over the years to aid me in my work for HABS/HAER.

J.E.B.
Washington, D.C.
July 1987

Preface
ROBERT KAPSCH

This book presents a selection of seventy-eight of the architectural photographs made by Jack Boucher over the last twenty-five years for the Historic American Buildings Survey (HABS), a division of the National Park Service. During the last third of those years, Jack has worked for me, and, with the publication of this book, it is only fitting that I try to add some framework to help the viewer to assess the significance of these extraordinarily fine architectural photographs.

At one level, Jack Boucher's photographs are intermingled with the general history and development of HABS. Begun in 1933 as a make-work project for unemployed architects, HABS continued after World War II documenting historic architecture through the use of measured drawings, large-format photographs, and histories. This material was deposited in the Library of Congress Prints and Photographs Division, where it was made available to scholars, researchers, and members of the general public—in fact, the HABS collection is one of the most widely used of the special collections in the Library of Congress. In the over fifty years of HABS's history, Jack Boucher has been the only full-time professional photographer regularly employed by the agency. In his career, Jack has created some fifty-five thousand large-format photographs of approximately six thousand historic structures—or over half of all of the large-format photographs in the HABS collection. All of these photographs are archivally processed, identified, and available to the public copyright free at the nominal cost of reproduction—representing an unprecedented archive on the growth and develop-

ment of American historic architecture.

At a second level, Jack's work has been used to define the national standards of excellence for the entire field of architectural photography of historic structures. HABS undertakes architectural photography, among other reasons, to assist in the preservation of important historic buildings. The American historic preservation movement is dedicated to, besides other goals, the preservation of the important visual values of architecture. Jack's photography is not only expected to technically capture the architectural image; it is also expected to assist in the process of defining these visual values. His photographs thus define the photographically achievable for historic preservation professionals working in the field.

Finally, and most importantly, Jack's photographs capture the vast range in the growth and development of American historic architecture. The illustrations in this book provide a small sampling of the American architectural heritage that has been bequeathed to all American citizens by the practitioners of this most public of arts.

This book does not mark the end of Jack Boucher's impressive career in architectural photography. Jack still undertakes a rigorous shooting schedule throughout the United States, traveling to numerous historic structures that need to be documented for the HABS collection. And his work will continue well into the future.

So I invite you to sample some of the highlights of twenty-five years of work dedicated to recording the finest buildings in the United States as captured by a master of his craft.

Contents

The Art of Architectural Photography
WILLIAM H. PIERSON, JR.

Jack Boucher is very special among architectural photographers. The greater part of his professional life has been devoted to recording American architecture for the Historic American Buildings Survey. This rare association with one agency has made necessary a dedication to purpose that to some might seem constraining; but not to Jack Boucher. For him it has been a vehicle to one of the most extraordinary photographic accomplishments of our time. He has experienced American architecture in a way that many architectural historians have not: he has examined with his own eyes every building he has recorded. He has walked around and through them all; he has savored their details. He has seen them under every condition of light and weather. Not until each has come alive for him through actual physical association has he lugged and lifted his large-format camera into place and composed and fine-focused the image. Every one of his photographs is touched by his unique sensitivity to the building as a living object inhabited by human beings. He has brought to his work that total commitment to a clearly defined and intelligently perceived objective that is the mark of all great artists.

Jack Boucher did not study architectural photography. Indeed, one would be hard pressed to think where he might have done so. He learned it from experience, by responding to the conditions of his assignments with a perceptive, probing eye and by mastering his craft in order to record and illuminate what his eye discovered. To him, buildings have never been subordinate elements to some larger pictorial design of his own. Instead, he has seen each as a design in its own right, and he has manipulated his camera to reveal and celebrate that design. This is what architectural photography is all about, and this is why Jack Boucher takes his place so easily among the leading architectural photographers in this country.

Jack Boucher's approach to architecture has always been conditioned by a fundamental relationship between the building and the camera: architecture is an art of three dimensions; the photographic print, on the other hand, is two dimensional, and like all pictorial art is therefore an illusion of space. It is an illusion, however, with a compelling sense of reality made possible by two functions of the camera, its optical system, which produces an absolute rendering of the complex geometric patterns of perspective, and the light sensitivity of the film, which captures with equal accuracy the tonal structure of the scene. In effect, the camera actually makes a tonal "drawing" of the building, and it is because of this that the English pioneer photographer William Talbot could properly call photography "The Pencil of Nature." Indeed, the word *photograph* means "light drawing." The photographer, however, has a distinct advantage over the draftsman: his image is based on the immutable laws of science rather than the vagaries of human observation and manual skill. The camera captures the appearance of a building exactly as it is down to the finest detail, and it was recognized from the beginning as the best instrument yet produced for the recording and study of architecture.

Jack Boucher's photographs are part of a long tradition in architectural photography that goes back to those early days. Indeed, the very first photograph ever made was architectural. Shot by Nicéphore Niépce in 1826, it shows a cluster of buildings as seen from an upper window of his home. From this blurred beginning architecture has continued to present an attractive subject for the camera. This is so because several physical aspects of both architecture and the camera make them particularly compatible. The most obvious of these is the simple fact that buildings do not move. This was a welcome advantage for the early photographers, whose cumbersome techniques required long exposures. It also facilitated small diaphragm openings that increased depth of field and assured greater sharpness, corner to corner; and where off-axis lens movements were involved, the small diaphragm made it possible to utilize the full covering power of the lens. In fact, the immobility of buildings is still advantageous, even with the high-speed films of today, especially for interior shots where low light situations make long exposures necessary.

There is another and more subtle relationship between object and camera that over time has made architecture such a challenging subject. Architecture is an art of geometry, and the main function of the camera is governed by the laws of optics, which are themselves geometric. Thus, a direct relationship exists between the camera and the building, and the effects of perspective, so essential to the illusion of three dimensionality, can be precisely recorded. Moreover, it did not take the early photographers long to discover that by manipulating the angle relationships between the film plane, the lens, and the object, both convergence and ellipsis could be predictably modified. The photographer was thus able to record a perspective image with absolute accuracy and at the same time to vary that image to enhance some spatial aspect of the building that to him might be important. In other words, the photographer had control of the image in such a way as to bring his own sensibilities to bear in the presentation and interpretation of the building.

Although the effects of perspective are constant, those of light are not. The quality, directness, and intensity of illumination vary to such a degree with time of day, camera position, and atmospheric conditions that it is highly unlikely that any two shots of the same building would ever be exactly the same. On the other hand, the photographer is free to choose his conditions of light. His expressive options are therefore substantially increased, particularly with respect to capturing the building in its most sympathetic luminous ambience. At the same time, the persuasive power of modeling—sometimes bold, sometimes discreet, at the photographer's option—can be made to reinforce the perspective image and reveal in controllable ways the three-dimensional geometry of the architecture.

The effect of light on the surface of objects, as recorded by the camera, also opened up a world of sensory experience that earlier graphic techniques had never been able to explore adequately. Light probed the peculiarities of surface to reveal texture, and the continuous tone of the camera image recorded that texture in faithful detail. In earlier graphic techniques, such as engraving, etching, mezzotint, even lithography, the texture of the technique itself was dominant, sometimes to the point of excluding altogether the textures of the object being recorded. The continuous tone of the properly exposed photograph, on the other hand, together with the capacity of the lens to render the smallest detail with infinite sharpness, brought to life the qualities of surfaces with a veracity that had eluded the printmakers. Roughness was now distinguishable from smoothness, and the tactile differences between various materials became immediately apparent.

Because it is geometric, architecture is an art of lines as well as planes and surfaces, lines defining shapes and delineating details, and all combining to create a specific set of proportions and a specific scale. It was in this area that the accuracy of the camera was so revolutionary, for it recorded things precisely as they were. In the earlier forms of graphic reproduction, proportion and scale, even though observed by the most discriminating eye and rendered by the most skillful hand, were, as often as not, subjectively recorded and even modified, both by the artist's intentions and by the peculiar qualities of the techniques being used. In Giovanni Piranesi's famous *Vedute,* for so long a primary source of information about the architecture of ancient Rome, buildings were made to seem taller or shorter, closer or farther away, simply by manipulating the proportions and the scale. As exciting as these brilliant images are, it is Piranesi's vision that we see and not an absolutely accurate recording of the buildings. By contrast, the truthfulness of the camera image was certain. Buildings from the past and from distant places were seen for the first time with consistent qualities of reality that led to wholly new directions in the study and interpretation of architecture.

Early books on architecture, beginning with the Renaissance and proliferating through the centuries to the time of the invention of photography, all presented images of buildings that were in some degree affected by the limitations and characteristics of their respective graphic techniques. From Serlio to Palladio to Piranesi, from Blondel to Boisseree to Viollet-le-Duc, from Gibbs to Adam to Pugin, and in this country from Benjamin to Downing to Sloan, the visual qualities of the illustrations—the sharp, often precise linearity, the various techniques for developing tone—were all more heavily infused with the individual mark of the illustrator than with that of the architect. Yet these visual characteristics had a direct effect on the architectural information communicated to the reader and ultimately left their imprint on the subsequent generations of architecture that these books influenced and sometimes even spawned. The vast majority of early American architects and builders, for example, knew the buildings that inspired their own work only from books. Thus, there are

qualities of flatness and thinness about many early American buildings that can be attributed directly to similar qualities in the flat, linear illustrations that formed their models.

The camera changed all that. With the development of the wet collodion plate process in the early 1850s, which rendered infinitely greater resolution and brilliance than the earlier paper negatives, architectural photography came into its own. In fact, except for portraiture, which would always have its poignant human appeal, photographs of buildings, or photographs with buildings in them, dominated the field for many years. Even though the collodion process required that the photographer take the developing paraphernalia directly into the field next to the camera, the early practitioners found a way, and the results were spectacular. Albums of architectural photographs began to appear, among them William Stillman's work on the Acropolis in Athens. Stillman was one of the earliest American architectural photographers, although he is probably better known to most American architectural historians as the founder of *The Crayon,* the first official journal of the American Institute of Architects.

Photographic studios that specialized in photographing art objects, including architecture, were also established in the major cities of Europe, particularly in Rome. Here the names of James Anderson and the brothers Alinari are especially prominent. All of these men, working with their large but flexible view cameras and slow but sharp lenses, demanded from the camera only what it could best give them: control of the perspective, continuity of tone, and high resolution of detail. It was the potential for accurate recording that fascinated them. Their approach to architecture was thus relatively innocent of any predetermined aesthetic values or any personal artistic intentions, and they made available to an eager and excited audience pure and unencumbered images that brought the solid geometry of architecture to life with a dramatic sense of presence. Indeed, the architectural photographs of these first true professionals are among the most compelling ever produced. Perhaps this is because the limitations of their youthful technology forced them to master fundamentals and to concentrate on those elements that solved the problems of architecture most directly, elements described by one contemporary critic as "the intelligent choice of the effects of light, purity of line (perspective), and transparency in the shadows (tone)" (the parenthetical comments are mine). By the 1860s, high-quality architectural photographs were readily available either through the photographers themselves or through dealers in the major cities, both in Europe and in the United States. Although architects still had their own libraries of architectural books and subscribed to the current architectural journals, they also began to collect photographs. In an era dominated by the eclectic mode of design, these photographs were an enormous asset, for they provided the architect with detailed information about the architecture of the past, information that had an accuracy and ready accessibility never available before. On the one hand, this reinforced the eclectic philosophy; on the other, it strengthened the architect's command over the basic elements of historical style. In the United States, the early growth of architectural photography coincided with the advent of the first architectural schools and contributed substantially to the growth of professionalism in this country. Richard Morris Hunt and Henry Hobson Richardson, both of whom had studied at the École des Beaux Arts in Paris and were thus central in bringing Beaux Arts methods of design to this country, had impressive collections of photographs that were available to both them and their assistants for reference and study. Hunt in particular, who was in Paris in the heady days when good architectural photographs were

first becoming available, had a large collection that he continued to expand over the years. There can be little doubt that the detailed architectural information contained in these photographs was a substantial factor in his versatile and authentic command of historical style. Although Hunt was one of the most traveled of American architects, had seen and sketched many of the most important buildings in the Western world, and had one of the largest architectural libraries in this country, it was his collection of photographs that provided the most accurate day-to-day data in his atelier.

There is one other slightly esoteric but nevertheless exciting relationship that developed with the advent of photography, and that was between the architectural photograph and architectural drawing. From the beginning the primary drawings of the architect have been the schematics, the drawings that show the dimensional part-to-part relationships of a building in exact measure and to scale. These are the plan, section, and elevation, which display the building in the horizontal and vertical plane and are entirely linear. From the point of view of establishing the configuration of the building inside and out they are all that is needed. Since a building is a three-dimensional object in a three-dimensional environment, however, the architect has always felt the need to present it as a full geometric presence, and here the perspective drawing was used. By the eighteenth century the mathematical principles governing perspective were thoroughly understood, and a three-dimensional, linear construct of the building, seen from a fixed position looking in a single direction, could be mathematically determined and exactly rendered.

Although a linear perspective drawing tells us everything we need to know about the geometry of a building, it tells us nothing about it as an object occupying space in a luminous environment. To accomplish this it was necessary for architects to develop also the tonal structure of the building, and to this end they turned to a long-standing device of the painter, light and shade. First thoroughly understood and analyzed by Leonardo da Vinci, the elements of light and shade—the light, the shadow, the shadow edge, and the reflected light—and their interaction with one another were rendered by the painter through any one of various continuous tone techniques. Of these, the one most closely associated with drawing was the watercolor wash. By the early nineteenth century architects were combining the fluid, descriptive power of the wash with the precision of the pen to create some of the most persuasive three-dimensional images found anywhere. The center of this style of drawing was the École des Beaux Arts in Paris, where it reached spectacular heights and began to take on an abstract purity that was the exact equivalent in tone to the linear absolutes of perspective drawing. The rhythmic continuous tones of the fluid washes brought to life the unencumbered planes of pure solids, flat and curved alike, and stripped them for the most part of any irregularities of surface. The effect of three dimensionality was stunning, but the delicate control of gradation through the wash reached such levels of perfection that the tonal image became as precise as the linear geometry, and the overall impression was thus as abstract as it was real. Again, technical virtuosity left its mark, frequently with breathtaking brilliance. The camera confirmed the logic of both the perspective drawing and the light-and-shade rendering. Endowed with the power to record the real, however, it also captured those qualities of surface and ambience that the wash could not easily reproduce. In an architectural photograph the building appeared as a living object, with real daylight articulating its surfaces and modeling its details. The camera also had the capacity to approach the building and isolate its smallest elements. The

photograph thus revealed the building not as an abstraction but as it actually was. For those who had relied on drawings and prints for their information about the architecture of the past, the photograph brought to their study a level of authenticity that could only be surpassed by an actual examination of the building itself.

Along with the differences between the architectural photograph and the three-dimensional architectural drawing, there is one point at which the two have a powerful affinity: in both, the building is seen from a single position, looked at from a single direction, at a single moment in time. Thus, since for structural reasons the principal lines of a building are vertical and horizontal, the line of sight is parallel to the horizontal plane and at right angles to the vertical. Because of the laws of optics, therefore, all parallel lines in the building that are at right angles to the line of sight will appear in the image (eye or camera) as parallel; those at an oblique angle will appear as converging. It follows that given a fixed horizontal direction of the line of sight, all vertical parallel lines, even in tall buildings, will be at right angles to the line of sight and will be seen as parallel, while all horizontal parallel lines that deviate from the right-angle relationship will be seen as converging. In like manner, all circles that lie in a plane at right angles to the line of sight will be seen as full circles; all those in a plane at an oblique angle will be seen as ellipses. Although other optical considerations affect the image, these are the primary facts about perspective that concern both the draftsman and the photographer.

In the architectural drawing the perspective is mathematically calculable, even when tall buildings are involved. With a camera, however, a tall building presents a problem. In some instances, it may be necessary to tilt the camera upward in order to include the entire building. This puts the line of sight at an oblique angle to the vertical plane and causes the vertical parallel lines to converge. In extreme cases, this can be very disturbing and can even make the building seem to be tipping over. The problem can be corrected by using a view camera equipped with the proper movements, either by tilting both the film plane and the lens board back to the vertical position, or by leaving the camera in a horizontal position and raising the lens to bring the building into the image field. Either way the basic angle relationships are maintained and the vertical parallels remain parallel. There are other movements of the camera that solve other optical problems, but "raising the front," as it is called, is the most common in architectural photography and was used very early in the history of the art. Except for more efficient and refined controls for performing the camera movements, the basic functions remain exactly the same, and a good view camera is still an essential tool for the serious architectural photographer.

During the second half of the nineteenth century, all the geometric capabilities of the camera were enhanced by advances in other areas of photographic technology. These included new emulsions with finer grain and greater speed; panchromatic emulsions, increasingly sensitive to the full color spectrum of light; improved lenses designed for a variety of functions; the development, with the advent of fast printing papers and electricity to provide sufficient light, of projection printing and the ability to make large prints from small negatives; the introduction of polycontrast papers that make it possible to apply different contrast ratios in different parts of the same print. All of these have given wider options to the architectural photographer.

On the other hand, one innovation that both strengthened and confounded architectural photography was the small, fixed-lens, hand-held camera. Made with a universal-focus lens and designed to accommodate roll film, so that several exposures could be made without changing film, these small cameras were intended for popular use to record the everyday events of life. Although handy and prolific, they had no immediate effect on serious architectural photography; not, that is, until the introduction of the Leica camera in 1926 and the subsequent development of 35mm photography. Designed to use motion-picture film and equipped with versatile, interchangeable lenses of superior quality, the 35mm camera offered advantages that attracted the professional as well as the amateur. With the addition of Kodachrome film in the 1930s and the 35mm projectable color transparency, all at an affordable price, a whole new world opened up for recording and disseminating information about architecture. Architects, architectural historians, and architectural critics began adding to their collections of black-and-white photographs the new and versatile color slides. In art departments throughout the country, the 35mm color slide began to supplement and finally replaced altogether the 3¼ x 4-inch black-and-white lantern slides that at one time formed the core of every academic slide collection.

The innovation that made the 35mm camera more effective as an architectural tool was the sliding-front lens. Although the conventional wide-angle lenses expanded the image field, and telephoto lenses pulled down details from inaccessible places, these were all fixed lenses and no adjustment of the perspective was possible. The sliding-front lens took care of that in part. When combined with a good telephoto lens, it made an attractive portable package with which to record architecture, both broadly and in minute detail, and still achieve a highly professional image; or so it seemed.

The truth is, the 35mm camera did not improve architectural photography, it redefined it, and it did so by imposing its own standards on those of established practice. It is obvious from the history of its development that the 35mm camera was not designed for architectural photography. In fact, its only concession to architecture since its inception has been the sliding-front lens, and even that has its limitations. The 35mm camera was and is intended to provide speed, flexibility, and the most sophisticated optical technology in a camera that is easy to handle and ready for instant action. It created the field of candid photography; it enormously extended the possibilities in photojournalism, sports photography, and nature photography; it brought to portraiture fresh qualities of informality and a sense of the moment. Above all, it put the latest in photographic technology into the hands of the eager amateur. In fact, the 35mm camera has become one of the most visible status symbols of modern life, as essential to the well-being of the average American as the hamburger and toothpaste. The number of amateur photographs that have been made since the invention of the Leica, a half-century ago, must be in the billions.

Even though it was not designed for that purpose, the 35mm camera has understandably been used for architectural photography. Indeed, it has grown so popular in that field that the large-format view camera is now regarded by many as a cumbersome, old-fashioned curiosity. The 35mm camera does seem to hold many advantages. Its ability to record quickly and in detail is unsurpassed by any other type of camera; it easily changes between black-and-white and color film; and it is the only type of camera that will handle the 35mm color transparency, now a standard and essential educational tool in this country. Combine that with the sliding-front lens, currently available from most leading manufacturers of 35mm cameras, and the advantages of the type for architecture are impressive.

Ironically, two of the basic qualities that make the 35mm camera seem so right for architectural photography, speed and ease of

handling, actually make it equally unsuitable. At the root of the problem is the high-speed lens. Because the 35mm camera was conceived as a hand-held camera that would function under minimal light conditions, speed has been a primary concern in lens design, and the principal means of achieving speed has been to increase the size of the aperture. Lenses with a stop factor of f/1.0 are now available. With the 1.0 factor, however, the diameter of the aperture is equal to the focal length of the lens, and since the focal length of a normal lens on a 35mm camera is 50mm, the diameter of the f/1.0 opening is actually larger than the image field itself. In terms of lens design this is a superb achievement, but the laws of optics are unyielding, and gain in one function of the lens leads inevitably to a loss in others. Unfortunately, those functions sacrificed to a large aperture are sharpness corner to corner across the image field and depth of field, both of which are absolutely essential to architectural photography.

Both corner-to-corner sharpness and depth of field can, of course, be increased by stopping down, but f/22 is now the smallest stop available in most lenses designed for the 35mm camera. Even my sliding-front lens, which is slow by 35mm standards (f/4), has a minimum diaphragm opening of f/22. By contrast, the 165mm lens for my 8 x 10 view camera is slower (f/8) but closes down three stops further to f/64. Proponents of the 35mm camera argue that f/22 is small enough for all practical purposes, and for most outdoor architectural shots this is true. For close-up work, however, where details are recorded in depth, and for interior shots where the depth of the image field is well inside infinity and is frequently measured in feet, the additional reach, both toward and away from the camera, that can be achieved with a small diaphragm opening is indispensable. So, too, is the increase in sharpness that the small opening extends to the extremities of the image field, a condition that is essential to the maximum movement of the sliding front.

When the 35mm camera is hand-held, which is what it was designed for, its effectiveness for architecture can be further jeopardized. Although the high-speed lens makes possible shutter speeds fast enough to eliminate the effects of hand movement, the small diaphragm openings necessary to achieve depth of field require commensurately slower shutter speeds, thus increasing the risk of hand movement affecting the sharpness of the image. Even more unfortunate, however, are the effects on the architectural image when a camera equipped with a sliding-front lens is hand-held. Because of the small size of the 35mm viewing screen, it is virtually impossible to compose the image, adjust the rise of the lens, and at the same time keep the camera absolutely vertical. One can come close, but close is not good enough, for even the slightest deviation from the vertical will produce some degree of convergence. Moreover, if that deviation is down instead of up, which can happen if the photographer is working too rapidly, the convergence is reversed, and the building seems to flare outward toward the top.

If it is difficult to achieve absolute verticality with a hand-held camera, it is virtually impossible to make and maintain the discrete adjustments in convergence that are frequently necessary. A tall building with regularly spaced parallel verticals or horizontals, for example, creates the optical illusion of divergence toward the top, and a photograph taken vertically will produce this same effect. The Greeks understood this phenomenon when, in building the Parthenon, they tilted the columns slightly inward to counteract that optical illusion. In such situations, however, the degree of distortion is generally very small, thus requiring adjustments so fine that they are only possible with a large-format view camera. With bubble levels and controls that make possible extremely delicate

adjustments, the angle relationships between film plane, lens axis, and the planes of the building can be refined with the utmost precision and then locked into place. Although camera stability can, of course, be achieved by using a tripod with a 35mm camera, the only adjustment currently available is the sliding front, and in this case the image in the viewfinder is too small to permit delicate control. In the end the lure of quick action almost always wins out, and the vast majority of 35mm architectural shots are hand-held, sometimes with disastrous results.

In view of the need for maximum sharpness in architectural photographs, another disadvantage of the 35mm camera is the small size of the working negative (24 x 35mm) it produces. Making an 8 x 10 print requires an eight-times enlargement, and even though modern fine-grain films have substantially reduced the effects of grain on the print, there is just enough increase in graininess in an 8 x 10 enlargement to take the edge off its crispness. In addition, 35mm film is roll film, and thus all the exposures on any given roll will be developed at the same time and to the same level of contrast. With the cut film of the view camera, each shot can be exposed according to the tonal structure of the subject and then individually developed to whatever contrast level will produce the desired results. In low light situations, for example, this technique makes it possible to expose for detail in the shadows and hold back the density of the lights by reducing the development time of the negative. In architectural photography, where details in both the lights and the shadows are desirable, this offers a reliable means of producing a negative that is rich in detail yet not too high in contrast.

Of all the innovations in 35mm photography, the most disturbing, as it relates to architecture, is automation. In such cameras shutter speed, diaphragm opening, and focus are all controlled by electronic sensors; the camera is programmed by a computer to respond to the scene in various modes, and an electric motor drive advances the film. All the photographer has to do is aim the camera and push the button; the machine does the rest. The result has been a flawless technical consistency that has freed the photographer to work with a confidence and speed never before possible. Everyone who owns such a camera is convinced that he or she is an expert. The truth is, the vast majority are not, especially in architectural photography. The electronic sensors are programmed to the average, not to the exceptional, and architectural photography presents many problems that cannot be solved on the basis of averages. Indeed, each building presents a unique set of conditions that requires the analytical power of human intelligence. In other words, it is the photographer who must make the decisions and not a machine.

It is the awesome prospect of having to make decisions that separates the architectural photographer from the photographer of buildings. To own a camera that is ready to shoot, without thought or preparation, is not only a way to avoid decisions but also compels one to shoot and shoot again. There are very few buildings, especially in the Western world, that have not been shot, from every angle and from every point of view, with every conceivable kind of lens, under every condition of light, and all with such predictable quality as to make the results indistinguishable one from the other.

In this frenetic world of compulsive, computerized frenzy, Jack Boucher's photographs stand out with stunning serenity. They are serene because they are contemplative. Boucher has approached every building he has ever photographed without arrogance and with a full realization that he is in the presence of a work of art. He has studied each building as an object in space, with camera in mind, but not in hand. He has analyzed the building's geometry, the rela-

tionships of its parts, its patterns of light and shade, its varieties of texture. Instead of walking and shooting, he has walked and thought and planned, so that before he goes through the laborious process of assembling his camera he knows where it must go and what light will be best for each camera location.

Because it is a sensory experience in time, architecture has been called frozen music, and it is precisely that, with one important qualification: in music the listener is fixed and the music moves, but in architecture the building remains still and the observer moves. Boucher is aware of this. He knows that human vision is a continuum of constantly changing binocular vignettes experienced in time, vignettes that are accumulated, sorted out, and collated by the brain into a total image in memory as well as in active sight. He is also keenly aware that, in contrast to the constantly shifting and focusing human eye, his camera stands solidly in a fixed position and sees through a single lens in a single direction at a single instant in time. Each of his photographs, therefore, must capture in a single image the salient elements of a continuous experience. To achieve this, he works first with those elements that evoke the illusion of three dimensionality, perspective, and light and shade. He also seeks out those that make the building a living object inhabited by human beings: its relationship with its environment, the flow and character of its interior spaces and their relationships with the exterior, the intimate specifics of detailing both as indicators of scale and as ornamental enrichment, the tactile quality of surfaces, and the inherent nature of materials. To relate all this to human vision, Boucher is aware that, because of the human eye's capacity to accommodate instantly to changes in focus and light intensity, the accumulative image that is communicated to the brain is sharp everywhere and rich in detail in the shadows as well as in the lights. Boucher's photographs, therefore, are as sharp as he can possibly make them. They are also exquisitely tonal, so that the smallest modulations of form are brought to life down to the minute variations of texture; and all of this is made possible not only through his mastery of that responsive and friendly instrument the view camera but also through his sensitive and intelligent work in the darkroom.

One school of photography today holds that creativity resides in the choice of subject, in the choice of moment, and in the aiming and shooting of the camera. It is only here, it is felt, that the photographer's special insights and sensitivities can be brought to bear. This is certainly true with respect to the automatic camera loaded with color film, for the camera's computer makes all the decisions concerning focus and exposure, and the inflexibility of the color chemistry makes any control in development virtually impossible. From the time of the exposure, the process is locked in by absolutes and the nature of the final print is predetermined. Some of the world's most famous photographers never touch their final prints but rely instead on outside laboratories to produce them; and there can be no question that the 35mm camera, with its speed, flexibility, and automation, lies at the center of this point of view. In the hands of genius, great photographs have been made this way. In the hands of lesser mortals, the result has been a sea of technically perfect dullness.

The other school of photography believes that, in addition to the work with the camera, the process of making the print also offers opportunities for creative thinking and management. This is even true in color printing where, in spite of the locked-in development process, decisions at the enlarger about exposure, filtration, and cropping do permit the imagination to affect the results. Black-and-white printing offers even greater flexibility, and with large-format negatives, shot and developed with specific printing techniques in mind, the possibilities for creative control are very sophisticated indeed. To be a part of a total creative act, however, the printing must be done by the photographer, not by someone else.

The photographs illustrated in this book were made by Jack Boucher and are the ultimate fulfillment of the thought process that began with his examination of the building, before his camera was even brought to bear, and did not end until the print was washed and dried. Given the differences between camera vision and human vision, and the fact that architecture can only be fully experienced in motion over time, these photographs capture with remarkable insights those aspects and elements of architecture that make it such an exciting art. They do so with simplicity and clarity and are a compelling testimony to Boucher's sensitive eye and his brilliant mastery of photographic technique. As in all great artistic performances, technique is the handmaiden of statement; in the end, it is the building as a work of art that Jack Boucher sees, understands, and celebrates.

The Historic American Buildings Survey
WILLIAM LEBOVICH

Photography has always been an integral part of the Historic American Buildings Survey (HABS), but staff photographer Jack E. Boucher has almost single-handedly elevated the importance of photography in HABS documentation. The work of Boucher and of the independent professional photographers employed by HABS often has a beauty and popularity rivaling that of the survey's measured drawings produced throughout the last fifty years.

The Historic American Buildings Survey was started in 1933 as a Civil Works Program, employing architects and architectural draftsmen and draftswomen to measure and draw significant American buildings from before the last quarter of the nineteenth century. The architects were also expected to write brief descriptions and histories of the properties being drawn. When the architect or draftsman was competent enough, he or she would also photograph the building; otherwise, if the budget permitted, a local professional photographer was hired. A surprising number of the architects and draftsmen were able to handle the bulky cameras, but very few of them were skilled enough to be hired as photographers.

On January 8, 1934, HABS issued Bulletin No. 11 entitled "Method of Securing Photographs," which articulated the policy toward photography and photographers:

In addition to the measured drawings it is desired to obtain photographs of each building measured. . . . The District Officers have the choice of employing professional photographers for the work, or of arranging to have the photographs taken by members of the measuring squad, if men are available among the measuring force who have the necessary experience and knowledge to insure that the photographs will be satisfactory for the purposes of record.

Bulletin No. 11 stated clearly the intended use for and character of photography: "The photographs are for purposes of record, so that it is more important that they be clear and sharp in their delineation of detail than that they be artistically composed or effective from a pictorial point of view. The photographer's station point, and the apertures, exposure and lighting, should be selected with this in mind."

Contrast that statement of photographic purpose with what the late Harley J. McKee wrote in HABS's *Recording Historic Buildings*, published in 1970:

Photographs of historic structures differ in character according to their purpose. Some are records, pure and simple; they are concerned chiefly with fidelity to form. Others establish a mood, or make a pattern of light and shadow which appeals to the viewer primarily as a creative design—a work of art. Architectural photography seeks to combine the best aspects of both. Fidelity to the subject is essential, of course, but it is a point of departure, not the entire objective. Architectural photography also makes use of a creative approach in order to add to the purely factual aspect of a picture, the intangible attributes which elevate "architecture" above "building." Some subjects are more responsive than others; it is not always possible to obtain more than a pure record but many times it is.

The work of Boucher and of contract architectural photographers such as Cervin Robinson, Cortland Van Dyke Hubbard, and William Barrett has demonstrated to the architects (and architectural historians) of HABS that, rather than diminishing the usefulness of the photographs as documents, aesthetic concerns can actually enhance the effectiveness of the photographs.

Boucher began his career with HABS in 1958. At that time HABS had recently been resuscitated and had neither standards nor policies for photography. He has been the agency's only full-time, permanent staff photographer. In addition, for the first ten years in the existence of the Historic American Engineering Record, from 1969 to 1978, he was its staff photographer as well. (The Historic American Engineering Record was spun off from HABS in 1969, and since 1978 it has had its own staff photographer.)

Jack Boucher's images were (and are) taken with large-format cameras, primarily 5 x 7 cameras. When it is impossible to use such a large camera, Boucher switches to a slightly smaller format, such as a 4 x 5 aerial camera for helicopter work and a 4 x 5 camera when working from a cherry picker. Large-format view cameras are used because of the excellent enlargements that can be made from the large negatives and the frequent need to enlarge miniscule areas of the photographs to study specific details, and because of the great degree of perspective correction they make possible. Boucher's personal preference for a 5 x 7 instead of the much more common 4 x 5 camera reflects his emphasis on quality and his conservative personality. HABS used 5 x 7 cameras in the beginning, so he still uses the 5 x 7.

It would be a disservice to the other fine architectural photographers who have done free-lance assignments for HABS to suggest that the broadened role for photography in HABS documentation is due solely to Jack Boucher. But the quantity and quality of Boucher's published images speak for themselves. The majority of the photographs in the already cited *Recording Historic Buildings,* the manual for documentation techniques, are his. The images in the Library of Congress exhibition entitled *A Record in Detail: The Architectural Photographs of Jack E. Boucher* and in this collection amply demonstrate his ability to convey the architectonic qualities of a building or building detail through aesthetically pleasing photographs.

To single out a few of the images included here, those of the porch at William M. Carson house (photograph 15), the gargoyle at the Healy Building (photograph 27), and the knocker at the David Ogden house (photograph 1) all suggest Boucher's unique vision and ability to create photographs that are informative, in a documentary sense, and have the movement or tension present in fine art photography.

Boucher's ability, as an architectural photographer, to balance the HABS requirements for documentary photography with his aesthetic sensitivities is a truly rare skill. Boucher's most mundane shots are still at a level of technical expertise that most photographs can only hope to reach, and even they are fine documentary photographs that meet the needs of the users of the HABS collection. When Boucher is able to elevate a documentary photograph to that higher plane of aesthetics—and his batting average is very impressive—he not only increases the pleasure of the users of HABS photographs, but he also significantly increases the numbers of users.

HABS documentation—whether the histories, measured drawings, or photographs—serves a variety of users. For some, the interest in HABS is very specific, very pragmatic. This is true for owners, restoration architects, or historians working on a particular building who want to use the HABS photographs, drawings, or data to aid in their research. Others have more general interests. One woman introduced a line of stationery featuring HABS drawings. Many people have a fondness for anything American and find the HABS collection a fascinating way to see this country and learn its architectural history. Scholars find the HABS collection an invaluable resource because it covers the entire country, because many of the documented buildings have been destroyed and are only known through HABS's resources, and because the high-quality photographs are free of copyright restrictions and are available for a reasonable charge that covers only the cost of reproduction. Very few books on American architectural history do not have at least some HABS photographs (usually taken by Jack Boucher).

It is this writer's impression that the photographs are the most frequently used and most often published part of the HABS collection at the Library of Congress. No statistics exist to support this impression, but the increase in the importance and popularity of photography over its originally intended role can be demonstrated in another way. Prior to 1986, HABS never had an exhibition dealing solely with photography, let alone showcasing the work of one photographer. Now the exhibition *A Record in Detail* and this accompanying collection of the photographs have recognized the work of Jack E. Boucher and implicitly recognized the importance of photography to the HABS collection.

Life Behind the Lens

JACK E. BOUCHER

As one interested in photographic history and the collection of related memorabilia, including books, I have been very aware of the meagerness of the accounts included in other photograph collections describing the adventures, problems, and equipment of photographers. When such an account does appear, it is usually a third-person report.

My role in the photographic scheme of things is miniscule indeed, and the accounts contained in the following article are modest compared to the exploits of the world's great photographers. But they are mine, and I offer them in all humility, accordingly. —JEB

Castillo de San Felipe del Morro looms, imposing and menacing, high above the waters at the entrance to the harbor of San Juan, Puerto Rico. Since the mid-sixteenth century, this enormous fortification has impressed seafarers, its stone ramparts towering above the tallest vessels able to enter the port. It is a masterwork of architecture and engineering—in my opinion, a fitting rival to any of the manmade wonders of the ancient or modern world. Arches and chambers, ramps and passageways honeycomb the structure; even today, under the peaceful administration of the National Park Service, "El Morro" evokes visions of pirates, square-riggers, treasure, and the Spanish Main, as well as feelings of admiration in those familiar with construction.

El Morro's design, construction, and history made it a candidate for documentation by the Historic American Buildings Survey (HABS), and in the latter part of the 1960s I landed in Old San Juan and set up my 5 x 7 view camera and some seven hundred pounds of equipment to record the fortress. My first photograph was of a sentry box reputed to be haunted, and a subsequent event tended to confirm that I had annoyed a guardian ghost.

The HABS Advisory Board had arranged the El Morro project in cooperation with the Instituto de Cultura Puertorriqueña to include more than a dozen structures in the area, about three weeks of work, including weekends. My wife, Peggy, accompanied me on the trip—at our own expense—and was of invaluable help as a photographer's aide, a role she has played countless times.

Each day following work, our time was our own, and we enjoyed our visit to historic Old San Juan. Late one afternoon, we set sail on a "sunset cruise on the 45-foot Catamaran 'MANGO.'" It was to be more than a pleasure sail—I wanted to see El Morro from the sea, to discover if there were any possibilities for photographing the structure from its most impressive side.

Under the circumstances I did not—could not—bring my camera, but my wife brought hers, a hand-wound Brownie 8mm movie camera. By the time we reached the harbor entrance and El Morro, the Brownie was in my hands, and I had retreated aft in the passenger compartment in order to photograph a submarine entering the harbor channel above water. About the same moment, other passengers' remarks regarding a wrecked freighter on the *other* side of the channel caused the crew member at the catamaran's helm to shift course, easing the craft across the channel—and across the path of the incoming submarine.

When the spring-wound Brownie ran down, the bow of the sub, seeming to loom as tall as El Morro but actually only some twenty feet above water, was eighty-eight feet from the starboard side of our catamaran. Just 4.2 seconds later, the sub made two twenty-two-and-a-half-foot catamarans out of our forty-five-foot vessel!

There is much more to the story, but space

14

is lacking to relate it here. Suffice to say no one was injured, everyone was drenched, the Brownie did not get wet, and the movie turned out wonderfully and was key evidence in an eventual court case involving the catamaran owner and the Navy. I never did get to examine or photograph the ramparts of El Morro.

I've opened my account of a quarter-century of HABS photography with this narrative for several reasons. It is but one of countless unusual experiences I have had as an employee of the National Park Service. The experience occurred during a necessary but innocuous aspect of an assignment, reconnoitering a structure to consider possible necessary views. (The "sunset cruise" was the easiest and most economical way to see the water exposures of the fort.) And it reflects my philosophy that (1) photography is a vital form of documentation, for my motion-picture film played an important part in the court case that resulted; (2) any photograph with any camera is better than none; and (3) a photographer must be ready to go to any length to "get the picture."

Atlantic City, New Jersey, was a fine place for a boy to grow up during the 1930s and '40s. The city was quiet and conservative with a lingering Victorian aura even into the war years, and many trappings of an earlier time remained to mold a mind and generate an understanding of the past and an enthusiasm to help preserve it that would manifest itself in the future.

Strollers on the famed boardwalk did not need to be reminded to wear shirts and shoes—they wore suits as well! Street vendors with pushcarts hawked fresh vegetables or fresh fish or fresh horseradish, ground and mixed while one waited. The iceman, using iron tongs, delivered blocks of ice to ice-boxes, and when I forgot my chore of emptying the pan under the icebox, the water overflowed and I had the privilege of clean-

ing the entire kitchen linoleum floor. The dairy was local, and the horse pulling the wagon knew every stop as the milkman delivered his glass bottles of milk.

Best of all were the transportation systems. Steam locomotives pulled passenger trains and freights to the Jersey shore until the mid-1950s; electric trolley cars plied the resort's main street till the end of the 1940s, not to mention the "Toonerville" interurban line to a neighboring shore resort.

My first camera was an early plastic Brownie 127 given to me when I was ten. When a freshman in high school, I was the only male member of an all-girl photographic club. My senior year, I worked as editor and photographer for the school paper.

One summer, at age sixteen, I worked for a photo shop on the Atlantic City boardwalk. It was an exceptional experience because of two of my responsibilities. I handled sheet and roll film developing using "dip-and-dunk" deep tanks, and, more importantly, I took photographs of people posed by me in the act of walking on the boardwalk, using a Graflex Super D 5 x 7 camera.

This was a camera that had been a favorite of professionals, especially newsmen, during the early years of the twentieth century, before it gave way to the more versatile Speed Graphic during the thirties and forties. It was a big hand-held camera, with a folding leather viewer that projected upward from the top ground glass to the photographer's eyes, and a brass-encased barrel lens nearly the size of a beer can that racked in and out as the cameraman focused. Shutter speeds were set on the focal plane shutter by winding two knobs to letter and numerical settings in order to attain the desired speed, and viewing was achieved via a reflex mirror similar to that in a 35mm SLR today but without the prism, since the image was simply reflected upward to a ground-glass screen.

Photographing people with this big camera during that late-1940s summer probably set my career in stone. I never had any doubt what I wanted to do in life from then on. Ironically, today I do not have the slightest interest in photographing people.

My first real job in photography was as a lab technician and engraver for a daily news-paper, the *Atlantic City Tribune,* where during a two-year tenure I wound up taking photo-graphs of everything from gaming raids, train wrecks, accident and murder scenes to ce-lebrities including Bob Hope, Jerry Colona, famed Danish tenor and metropolitan opera star Lauritz Melchior, and others.

A hurricane struck in November of 1950, and Atlantic City's streets were inundated. Bridges were damaged or destroyed; the rail line to the resort washed out, the boardwalk washed away in areas—and I was the only professional photographer out in the ele-ments photographing the havoc, at times by boat, at times literally up to my armpits in swirling waters holding my 4 x 5 Speed Graphic over my head. But my photographs filled a double truck (two pages) plus the front page of the *Tribune,* and a box headline said simply, "Jack's Camera Kept Clicking."

When the newspaper sold out to a compet-ing daily for which my father was employed as a staff reporter—and which had a rule against father and son combos—I sought and landed a job as lab technician and photo as-sistant for Fred Hess & Son Photographers of Atlantic City. It was a priceless experience. As a newspaper photographer, I had used only a 4 x 5 Speed Graphic. But during my two-year stint with Hess Studios I gained inti-mate experience with view cameras, both 8 x 10 and 12 x 20 banquet cameras as well as 4 x 5 press cameras and the panoramic circuit cameras. And I made my first aerial photographs. Hess Studio's photo lab de-manded quality work—if I made two hundred 8 x 10 enlargements from a single negative, the first print had to match the last one flawlessly, and the prints had to be of salon quality.

In the early fifties, New Jersey began to make plans to build the proposed 172-mile-long Garden State Parkway to serve the shore resorts, and the word was out that the state was looking for a photographer. My applica-tion was accepted, and I became one of the project's first dozen or so employees in 1952. It was a four-year experience that was almost exclusively architectural and engineering in nature. I rode crane buckets to the tops of 150-foot booms and girders being placed into position atop 135-foot-tall piers, all with a 4 x 5 Graphic in one hand. At this time, the 35mm camera was still strictly for amateurs. In fact, the 4 x 5 was regarded by many then as medium format.

My interest in architecture and history, which dates to building a model of the Tem-ple at Karnak in school, was greatly en-hanced by my work for the Parkway. For the Parkway's public-relations activities I photo-graphed countless historic structures and sites along its route, often writing articles to ac-company my photographs. In my spare time I roamed the Jersey Pine Barrens, photograph-ing houses and villages, old churches and the remains of iron furnaces, mills and bridges.

A year after the Parkway's final section opened to the public, there was little left for me to do, and I had begun seeking a job that would combine my interests in photography and in history when a friend suggested the National Park Service. George Grant, distin-guished pioneer photographer for the Park Service, had retired in 1954. The Service had tried for four years to exist without replacing him, depending on photos of varying quality sent in from their field areas. The result left much to be desired.

But the Service had instituted Mission 66, a ten-year program to rehabilitate the Park System by 1966, and it reconstituted the His-toric American Buildings Survey, which had been moribund since the war years. HABS needed a photographer, and by chance I ap-plied at that moment. My nine years of experience, all by coincidence oriented toward their needs, uniquely qualified me, and I was hired. I was assigned to work jointly with the Washington Branch of Still and Motion Pictures under Ralph A. Anderson, Chief of the Branch and a fine photographer, and Charles E. Peterson, Chief of Historic Structures at the Eastern Office of Design and Construction in Philadelphia, and majordomo of HABS.

A one-month-long field trip through the Southeast accompanied by Park Service historic architect Roger Jones (who I found out much later was along to observe me) became unforgettable when, in the midst of an assignment to make photographs from a helicopter at Jamestown Island in Virginia, our chopper lost power for several moments, dropping a couple hundred feet before the pilot was able to get the engine running again. He assured me he still had enough altitude to auto-rotate to safety, but I'm still a bit skeptical to this day. He headed back to base, posthaste.

A photographer's lot is really a happy one. There is a necessary mixture of office and field work, so it is never really possible to become weary of either. Photography cannot be done behind a desk; yet, like any government employee, I have my share of paperwork—orders for equipment and supplies, travel authorizations, and vouchers to be paid for my expenses, or at least most of them, maximum rates in government being what they are. Per diem when I first traveled for the Service in 1958 was $12.00 for lodging and food and $.07 per mile for a car. I can recall walking out of a motel in New England that wanted to—as we say in the eighties—"rip me off" for $7.50 per night. Today, a per diem of $126.00 in New York City and $.20½ per mile is not adequate.

But the rewards more than compensate. There is the satisfaction of working with an organization staffed with knowledgeable specialists committed to their professions and dedicated to their organization. Even today,

an esprit de corps still exists despite prevalent but unwarranted criticism of the federal service in general. And for me, as photographer for the National Park Service's unique HABS program, there is the interest and excitement of being able to go behind the scenes, not only in the national parks but also in the historic structures of America to see "how they tick" and to photograph the "works."

It was not unusual during my early years with the Service for me to leave Washington or Philadelphia on a multiple field assignment that would last three months. One trip, of thirteen thousand miles through the West, lasted five months. I took three days off during this period and felt guilty for doing so.

It was during one such three-month assignment in the early 1960s that I arrived in New Mexico. I was to record the inscriptions left on the rocky mountainsides of another El Morro, the El Morro National Monument in New Mexico, by the conquistadors during the sixteenth century and by later explorers.

Arriving in unfamiliar territory late in the day, territory as desolate and unsettled as any in the West, I stopped at a building that had once been a roadside store and would have done credit to any movie set. There had been no other structure for countless miles, and I needed directions. The door was locked, and I knocked. The man who opened the door had a face that reminded me of the portraits on a post office wall. He seemed to tower above me as tall as the doorway, which resulted in the business end of the 30.06 rifle cradled in his arms being pointed just about at my chest area. Swallowing a slight uneasiness, I simply said I'd like some directions. He did direct me to El Morro, and I left, wondering to what altitudes my blood pressure had soared.

There were no accommodations at El Morro, or within sixty miles or so via the gravel road I had been traveling, so I camped for the night under the stars after preparing a modest dinner. I don't know how long I had been asleep, what caused me to awake, or what the time was, but I heard a slight noise nearby in the coarse gravel . . . and another noise . . . and then silence. With the memory of the not-too-friendly chap with the 30.06 rifle fresh in my mind, and his place only a few miles distant, I froze, not daring to move even for a glance at my watch.

From my sleeping bag, I could see little but treetops and the bright moon above. I heard the noise again—it did sound like a footstep. Then again, but this time there was a bump at the bottom of my sleeping bag, yet I could see no figure standing over me. Turning my head slowly to the side I could see the source of the noises in the moonlight. There was no 30.06, but the threat was considerable. Not five feet away, fortunately looking away from me, was the biggest civet cat I had ever seen. A member of the skunk family, he could have made the night far more memorable had I scared him. I'd have been a week getting rid of the aroma. When he left, finally, I had a triple shot of brandy from my first-aid kit (that was all it contained) and crawled back into my sleeping bag.

Upon arriving in the morning at the headquarters of El Morro National Monument, I learned that Yellowstone National Park had been struck by a strong, violent earthquake. The quake, registering high on the Richter Scale, had been felt throughout the American Northwest, and radio reports indicated the epicenter was within a few miles of Old Faithful geyser. A mountain had tumbled, causing landslides to crash into a campsite burying an unknown number of campers. I notified the Washington office of my whereabouts, and soon a call came through directing me to proceed to Yellowstone immediately to document the damage. It was about eight hundred miles, but I was there the next morning.

Using my 5 x 7 (then a Deardorff), my 4 x 5 Speed Graphic, and a 35mm Leica (for lecture slides only), I recorded a scene of

great devastation. Rockslides had covered roads, and bridges were down or damaged. Rescue operations were underway at the buried campsite, but many campers were dead. I was in the air for four hours making low-altitude aerial photos with my 4 x 5. Shooting 1/400 of a second at f/8 on 400 ASA film with a G filter gave me fine results. When I left Yellowstone some seventeen days later, the ground was still shaking with occasional aftershocks.

Later, in California, I joined with architect Charles Pope of the Western Office of Design and Construction for the Park Service, who, among many other activities, was overseeing HABS work in California. Together we traveled through the state for a month documenting some of the missions. At night, in our spare time, Pope, who like myself is a licensed radio amateur, relaxed by using the 60 watt all-band transmitter in my car to chat with fellow "hams" around the country and in Canada and Mexico.

Not long after my return East, I was sent to South Carolina to record structures in Columbia and Stateburg. At Stateburg, my assignment was to record a beautiful Gothic Revival church, the Church of the Holy Cross (see photographs 22-23), and an eighteenth-century plantation home, the Borough House, both built of "pise de terre," or "rammed earth."

Not until a quarter-century later was I to return to Borough House, in 1986, to do further, far more extensive documentation as part of an assignment to record other architecture in South Carolina. That assignment was the result of the efforts of HABS staff member Richard Anderson, a historic architect and native South Carolinian. Borough House is and has been the family home of Richard and the Anderson family since the eighteenth century. Had Richard been at home when I was there in the 1960s, neither of us would have ever suspected that the preteen and I would one day be colleagues in HABS. It is a small world indeed.

But there is more to the story of that original trip. After I left Borough House, I traveled a dozen miles to the village of Pinewood to record the remains of Milford Plantation, home during the Civil War era of John Manning, a pre–Civil War governor of South Carolina (see photographs 56–59). Leaving the paved road, I drove with Jim Massey, then Chief of HABS, down a long gravel drive, lined on both sides with oaks, all dripping with Spanish moss. We suddenly emerged into a clearing to see the ornate rear of a once magnificent three-story plantation house. Palladianesque wings reached around us from the main house. The portico of the house was magnificent. Three-story-tall columns with Corinthian capitals supported the roof, and the whole overlooked a broad expanse of long, unkempt lawn. Milford had been long abandoned. I recall open windows and a virtually empty interior. We had been warned that the plantation was uncared for and its future dim.

It took a day and a half to make adequate coverage for HABS. Because I had Jim Massey with me, I was able to photograph the interior by painting with light, a favorite technique. If a room has a fair amount of ambient light illuminating it, I like to use this as my base lighting and simply bounce additional light from a big flashbulb off the wall and ceiling behind me to lighten shadows.

The flashbulbs I used at the time were General Electric #22s and #50s. The #50 bulb was about the size of a 200 watt standard electric lamp, and the #22 a bit smaller. Both had light output far in excess of the 200 watts/second electronic strobe light, then and now the strongest portable electronic flash available. (One or two brands of strobes now claim outputs of 400 watts/second—still far, far short of the output of these flashbulbs.) Today, such bulbs are made only by GTE Sylvania, all other American manufacturers

sadly having ceased to manufacture them. GTE's bulbs are designated #2 and #3.

The trick in such interior photography is to light adjacent rooms that open into the room being photographed, so that these spaces do not appear dark or black. Extension flashes can be rigged using long cords to the camera flash-control unit, but these take time to run and are usually difficult to conceal.

Accordingly, we painted with light. I'd withdraw the dark slide after placing the film holder in the camera and setting the shutter. Massey, acting as my assistant, held the dark slide directly covering the lens and almost touching the metal mount surrounding the lens. At my command "up," he would raise the slide clear of the lens, I would flash one bulb in a desired direction to illuminate either a dark area of the room being photographed or an adjacent room. When he saw the flash, Massey would replace the slide over the lens, and we would repeat the series of actions as many times as necessary to light the entire scene, including any back- or highlighting desired. I'd use the smaller electronic flash when the area to be illuminated was small. Some photographs have required dozens of such flashes. In this case, the result was a pleasingly exposed photograph that would not have been possible without an assistant.

Had there been electricity in the house, I might have used flood lamps, but this is often both difficult and potentially very unsafe in photographing a historic house, especially with today's quartz lamps ranging in brilliance to a thousand watts. Many old houses still have their original wiring, which is usually fused for 15 amps. Three quartz lamps of 600 watts each equal 18 amps, enough to overload a circuit and at the least blow a fuse or, if the panel has been modernized, trip a circuit breaker. If a careless homeowner has had a problem with blown fuses, it is highly likely that, in ignorance, he has replaced fuses with ones of higher ratings. This overloads wires and can easily result in a fire should the photographer try to run three or four quartz lights. Thus, a knowledge of electricity can be essential for the photographer.

We moved through Milford Plantation photographing what had been a most glorious house. Among the scant furnishings were two enormous Empire bookcases about twelve or fourteen feet tall. These were nearly lost in the rooms, which had ceilings about five feet taller yet. I often wonder in such circumstances what I would learn if the walls could speak; what treasures lie hidden, perhaps under the floorboards beneath my feet. This time I would find out, but not until years later.

A few years passed. A phone call came into the HABS office from South Carolina, from Milford Plantation. A couple from Detroit, Michigan, Mr. and Mrs. W. R. Clark, descendants of Governor Manning, had taken over Milford and restored it. They had received a set of the HABS photographs I had made and now, with Milford restored to her former glory, wanted me to return at their expense and rephotograph it. I did. And learned of the treasure that had been hidden within inches of me when I was there.

I spent three magnificent days as their guest, recording the restored plantation house and dependencies. Hanging on the second-floor wall was the treasure of Milford, found when the new owners moved and discarded those huge Empire bookcases. Behind one had been a yellowed roll of paper. Revealed, when it was unrolled for the first time since it had been hidden during the Civil War, signed by some 145 members of the South Carolina legislature, 25 others, and the governor, was the only known mint-condition copy of the Ordinance of Secession, the one document that could be said to have started the Civil War.

HABS up to this time had been headquartered in Philadelphia, and I lived an hour's drive distant near Atlantic City. As a New Jersey resident and near native (born in Buffalo, New York), I was deeply interested in Jersey history and active in historic-preservation circles, all very compatible with my HABS duties. I had written four books relating to various aspects of Jersey history; had been chairman of a state-appointed group aiding in the preservation of an eighteenth-century iron furnace village, Batsto; was president of the six-hundred-member Atlantic County Historical Society; and had been primarily responsible for the preservation and stabilization of another iron furnace and paper mill ruin, Weymouth. I was also responsible for the preservation and restoration of Atlantic City's 1857 Absecon Lighthouse and helped in the preservation of the famed architectural folly "Lucy," the Margate Elephant. And there were other activities.

Doubtless because of this involvement, I was offered a position directing the New Jersey Office of Historic Sites, which I declined because it was nonphotographic. However, about this time, rumors that HABS's offices would move from Philadelphia to Washington materialized. To remain with the National Park Service and HABS, I would have to move to the Capital, something that, at that time, would have been very inconvenient. After some further hesitation, I resigned from the Park Service and accepted the New Jersey position.

A frustrating three years and several months later, I finally gave up and resigned the Jersey position to return to photography, which I had not altogether ignored while with the Garden State. I set up a laboratory and began accepting contracts to record historic structures for the federal government and various states. In short order, I was kept busy by the Park Service and HABS. The Historic American Engineering Record (HAER) was established in 1969, and James C. Massey, Chief of HABS and now also of HAER, offered me my old job back, which I accepted easily because of my reinstatement rights. It was good to again be part of the National Park Service team and the HABS/HAER programs.

Probably the single question I am most frequently asked is, "What style or type of building do you most enjoy photographing?" My answer is simple. I always feel that whatever building I am photographing at a given moment is the most important structure I have ever been assigned. I've photographed well over six thousand structures for HABS and HAER, buildings from privies to palaces, and I have as much enthusiasm for the vernacular log cabin as I have for a grand Newport mansion.

It is important to have this outlook. As photographer for HABS, I never know when I make a photograph where or when it will be used. My photographs have appeared in hundreds of books, magazines, and journals illustrating articles by people who are total strangers to me. Their needs, satisfied by the collections of HABS and HAER, are as diverse as is the architecture of America itself. So I believe in doing the best job of which I am capable. How often I succeed is for others to judge.

I firmly believe there are three factors essential to success in photography: (1) knowledge, of both photography and the subject matter; (2) equipment, including the finest cameras, lenses, meters, and related items; and (3) a laboratory, since a successful photographer must process his own films and make his own prints.

The need to know, to understand photography is obvious, but the need to have a working knowledge of the subject is perhaps less apparent but equally vital. Pity the sculptor of the human form who lacks an understanding of anatomy. To enhance my understanding of architecture and architectural history I've taken, in addition to workshops and seminars in this country, special courses such

as the Attingham Summer School offered in England by Britain's National Trust, and the European Traveling Summer School for Restorationists developed on a one-time basis by Charles E. Peterson, FAIA, and directed by W. Brown Morton, noted restoration consultant.

Equipment cannot be compromised; quality affects performance. Inferior lenses, undependable shutters, unstable tripods, blind meters, and more all take their toll on the quality of the image being produced. But the best quality equipment is not always the most expensive or the most elaborate.

Finally, there is the laboratory. The photographer who does not process and print at least a majority of his work loses his system of checks and balances. By this I mean that the making of the negative and print in the lab provides a basis for refining photographic field techniques. Many a superb negative has been ruined by a poor lab technician in printing; many a poor negative has been salvaged by a skilled lab technician.

So strongly have I felt on this latter point that for a dozen years I used my personal laboratory for my government HABS/HAER work, underwriting the enormous cost of this personally. At present, HABS does not have a photographic laboratory but must farm its work out to a low bidder. The firm does above-average work and is most cooperative, but HABS photographic quality suffers in general, and the cost to the government of this approach is excessive.

Some half-dozen years ago the HABS/HAER programs had developed to the point that one photographer could not possibly handle all the photographic assignments. Accordingly, HAER retained a staff photographer, Jet Lowe, who has proved to be an accomplished lensman and a dedicated participant in the agency's activities. On occasion, for efficiency and economics, he'll undertake a HABS assignment or I'll handle a HAER assignment.

HABS (and HAER) photography is normally a land-based operation, in that all the documentation is done in and around a structure (building) or feature (canal, railroad, and so forth). But there are exceptions that call for special treatment, notably aerial photography. Historic districts, farm complexes, canals, railroads and railyards, and more demand aerial photography as part of the documentation. Only through this medium can the working relationship of structures and features be documented and comprehended. The reader will recall my comments discussing helicopter photography over Jamestown, Virginia, and over Yellowstone Park. Regardless, the "chopper" remains the most satisfactory method of making aerial photographs. It is tantamount to portrait photography; in fact, I like to call it aerial portraiture. I have spent more than eight hundred hours taking aerial photographs.

I prefer small choppers such as the "Jet Ranger," a four-seater craft with a cruising speed somewhere around 140 mph or more and with adequate power to hover just about motionless at my favorite photographic altitudes, which vary slightly depending on the area to be photographed. Generally, I find between 150 feet and 600 feet to be the best altitude for photography, although I've had to instruct the pilot to go as high as 2,500 feet on an assignment to photograph the Lucin Cut-Off, an eleven-and-a-half-mile-long wood rail trestle across the Great Salt Lake in Utah.

Always, I have the door removed from the aircraft and sit either on the seat along the open door or cross-legged on the floor at the opening. A dependable seat belt is essential and intercom connection with the pilot very important. This type of photography becomes aerial portraiture because the photographer using a chopper can *request* the pilot to stop (hover), move back, move right, move left, go up or down, and so forth. And legal altitudes for a helicopter are far lower than those

for fixed-wing aircraft such as Piper Cubs and similar craft. In addition, fixed-wing craft must maneuver into position, while the photographer hopes to arrive at the camera point correctly and when the sun has not gone behind a cloud. In this gymnastic-like process, the occasional fixed-wing aerial photographer needs to supplement his photo equipment inventory with a barf bag.

I use my Linhof 4 x 5 Super Technika with a Schneider Symmar 150mm focal length lens for small aerial assignments where there are only a few dozen photographs to be made. For more extensive projects I share with HAER photographer Lowe a World War II "K-20" Army aerial camera. We would both like to have a fine Linhof Aero-Technika, but the camera is beyond the office budget and could not be justified on the basis of need.

"Extraordinary" best describes a three-day assignment to record the historic structures along the route of the old Erie Railroad in New York State in 1971. Using a ten-seat Huey helicopter furnished by the state of New York, a crew of five of us in addition to the pilot and co-pilot flew the Erie road at an average altitude of 250 feet above the tracks. Our journey took us from the Hudson River to Lake Erie across the lower tier of the state, then north along Lake Erie and back across the northern tier of the state, following trunk lines where they could be located. Photographs were keyed to U.S. Geological Survey quad sheets for identification.

The trip required twenty-seven hours of flying time, about nine hours a day. Working together during the flight were Robert Vogel, Curator of Mechanical & Civil Engineering for the Smithsonian Institution; Jack Waite, then Senior Historic Architect for the New York State Historic Trust; Chester Leibs, then Senior Historian for the Trust; Eric DeLony, Senior Architect (now Chief) for HAER; and myself. It was the first major undertaking of this sort for the new Historic American Engineering Record, and my colleagues alternated as spotters, map readers, and recorders, shooting color slides and helping me to reload film. The aerial survey was followed up by conventional ground photography.

HABS/HAER photography is exclusively large format, in black and white. Every effort is made to correct for perspective distortion well within one degree, to reveal maximum structural detail, and to provide a document—the film negative—that will, with archival developing and storage, last approximately five hundred years. New techniques should be discovered by that time that will prolong the film's life ad infinitum.

After the camera is set up for a photograph, and the black-and-white exposure made, and if both the structure and the composition are worthy, I may make a color transparency for use when needed and for as long as it lasts without appreciable fading. Seldom is more than one view of a structure made in color, and the transparency, because of its temporal nature, does not become a part of the HABS (or HAER) archive. The availability of these color transparencies, which represent only a small part of our photographic effort, has enhanced the viability of the HABS/HAER collection to a vast degree. Authors and publishers especially have found the color transparencies useful in illustrating articles for publication.

Five by seven inches has been the standard HABS/HAER format since both programs were founded, and it remains the standard for good reasons. The relatively large 5 x 7 negative can be contact printed easily and the print dodged to some extent with the resulting image sufficiently large to be of value, and film grain that might otherwise obscure detail is not a problem. Small details in a 5 x 7 negative can be greatly enlarged for examination, whereas they would be lost in the grain in a 35mm or 2¼ x 2¼ negative. View cameras are not available in a format smaller than 4 x 5 inches, and the 4 x 5 format is the

smallest HABS/HAER will accept. I'd be delighted to work again in 8 x 10, but the equipment for shooting this size of film is more cumbersome, and film and developing costs would double.

Today I use a Linhof 5 x 7 Master TL view camera with an assortment of lenses, mostly Schneiders, ranging from 90mm to 508mm, the latter being an ancient Bausch & Lomb mounted in an equally ancient Betax #3 shutter. A top-of-the-line, maximum-size Gitzo tripod with elevator center post and a Gosson Ultra Pro meter, a Norman 200B electronic flash, and Smith-Victor quartz lamps head the equipment inventory.

My twelve Fibrebilt padded cases transport now about nine hundred pounds of equipment and supplies designed to satisfy every eventuality. There are Tiffen filters and Tote-A-Lites; tools for field repairs; and spare batteries, cable releases, quartz bulbs, and flashbulbs. There is a case lined with thin lead sheeting for transporting all film both unexposed and exposed, as well as telescoping Leitz scale sticks to include in selected views to reveal scale to researchers.

I also always carry forty-inch-by-eight-foot lengths of rubberized black photographic cloth and inch-wide Scotch black photo tape. Using these two items I can seal off a motel bathroom in minutes to improvise a darkroom for changing film, even in the middle of the day. But it is always necessary to wait an absolute minimum of twenty minutes in the total dark to check the room for light leaks, which can materialize around electric fixtures, air vents, and plumbing. It is essential even to watch for the afterglow of fluorescent tubes. I remove my luminous dial watch before handling film.

Any discussion relating to photography must include film and chemistry. Personally, I prefer Kodak products for a number of reasons. They have consistently performed well, are readily available, and cover a wide range of needs. But probably most important is the fact that when and if a problem arises, it can be resolved quickly, through immediate reference to any of Kodak's enormous quantity of published literature, through a toll-free phonecall, or through a personal visit by one of Kodak's corps of tech-reps.

Royal Pan film, with an exposure index of 400 ASA, has been my black-and-white choice for years, although I am at this writing experimenting with the new TMAX film that also has an ASA rating of 400. I've standardized on *HC-110* developer, although there will be a special developer for the TMAX film. The relatively small amount of color photography I shoot for HABS is done on Ektachrome sheet film, E-6 process, and the film is machine processed.

Our HABS/HAER standards are very strict regarding film processing because of the vital importance of archival stability. We are shooting for posterity, striving to attain the longest possible life for our photographs. Sadly, no one will venture to define specifically the term *archival stability,* not even two of the premier document conservation organizations, the American National Standards Institute or the Library of Congress.

To attain the hypothetical goal of five hundred years longevity, black-and-white films must not be machine processed; they must be "souped" by hand in the traditional "dip-and-dunk" method, then washed in running water, treated in a "hypo" neutralizing agent, washed again in running water, and then given a final bath in a wetting agent before drying, all for proscribed times well in excess of those recommended. Developed films are immediately placed in acid-free Mylar sleeves until final filing in acid-free envelopes and storage in metal cases maintained in a climate-controlled atmosphere.

Prints must be made on rag-based paper if archival stability is of concern and processed similarly to the film. It can be argued that the film—that is, the negative and not the print—is the vital document. However, no crystal ball will reveal a photographic print's long-term future. If a print has been properly processed it may last half a millennium, more or less, and at some point provide a scholar with a priceless record that might otherwise not exist. Most of the nineteenth-century prints surviving today meet these criteria.

I've used the bathroom lab in the field since my first assignment. Sheet film must be reloaded into and out of holders each night so the photographer is fully prepared for the next day's shooting. Large-format photography is not as convenient as small-format roll-film picture-making. At least one no longer has to coat a glass plate with collodion, rush it without any exposure to light from a dark tent to the camera, and then rush it back again to the tent for development after taking a multisecond or even full-minute exposure, as my nineteenth-century predecessors did.

Admittedly, in my early days of travel with the Park Service and HABS, I did try to develop my film each night after the day's labors. While this was very useful on the long three-month trips, occasional problems with hard or soft water, unfiltered dirty water, temperature control, and other such niceties caused me to abandon this exhausting effort which made for fifteen-hour workdays.

My modus operandi in documenting a structure for HABS/HAER begins with an elevation view of the main facade of the structure to be recorded. I make sure that the camera back is as parallel both vertically and horizontally to the plane of the facade as the instrument permits. One view is made with a fourteen-foot-long scale stick, with one-foot increments marked in red and white, laid adjacent to the subject, and one view is made with the stick removed.

Then I make a perspective view of the main facade that will also include one side. The view and angle chosen depend on the visibility of details and aesthetic considerations. Then I make as many other general and detail views as I determine are necessary to interpret the structure and record it. Six or eight exterior views are usually adequate for an average two-and-a-half-story single-family residence.

Inside, I may make about three photographs: a stairhall with perhaps a detail of a balustrade or a newel post; a general view of the principal room; and/or a detail of a fireplace and mantel. Regardless, I check the house from cellar to garret for original architectural details.

But coverage can be far more extensive. About one hundred photos each were necessary to record Cliveden and Andalusia, houses in the Philadelphia area. In May 1987 I made 151 photographs of the dependencies *alone* of Scotty's Castle in Death Valley, California. I'll not be recording the Castle itself for another year, but it will require at least one hundred views, so rich is it in detail.

I have, therefore, two approaches in documentation, and which one I employ depends on the extent to which I intend to record the structure. If the coverage is to be minimum, of a dozen or less photographs, I'll simply pick and choose those details that I consider significant, reflecting style and construction with possibly an extreme close-up of a detail included. However, in the case of a major structure where I am to shoot dozens or even more than a hundred photographs, this approach is enlarged upon. I'll make photographs to interpret design features as completely as possible and to relate features to one another and to the structure.

Fallingwater, Frank Lloyd Wright's Pennsylvania masterpiece, is a good example (see photographs 40–49). The house is built over a waterfall, and a stairway with a landing leads up from the stream above the fall into the principal room, the living room. Doors and sliding windows enable the homeowner to open this stair wide to the living room. During warm weather, this adds the cooling

element of stream-cooled air to the house and provides easy access to the stream for viewing.

After recording the living room and showing this access in a portion of the photograph, I recorded only the access area in a closed configuration. Without moving the camera, I then opened doors and sliding windows and rephotographed the same scene. (There have been times when I have made deliberate double exposures, to show movement of a door, window, or other detail on a single sheet of film.) Then, taking equipment outside, and down to stream level, I made photographs to show the staircase, the landing, and their relationship to the stream. The result is that the entire story of this one significant detail has been documented.

Photography of the Hagan house (see photographs 11–13) was the result of a chance conversation between myself and the curator of Fallingwater. HABS was unaware of the existence of another Wright house only ten miles from Fallingwater. It made no sense to pass it up since it was so close to my assignment. Importantly, the original owners, who still occupied the house, were in residence. I recorded the house, which was of radically different design from Fallingwater, in considerable detail.

Six months later the house was sold and its owners for the thirty years of its existence moved. A couple of months after that, during some minor work by the new owner, the house burnt, destroying, I understand, at least half the original fabric. HABS photos were the best and only accurate pictorial record of what had existed, and they have been a major aid in the restoration of the house.

Greek Revival is the prevailing style of north-central New York State and to my mind is relatively simplistic compared to earlier or later influences. Hence, when I arrived at the Joseph Morse house in Eaton Village, New York (see photographs 36–39), I was unprepared for several unusual, indeed unique, features. One never does know what to expect on an assignment, and therefore it is virtually impossible to plan the length of individual projects.

There was a very fine latch on the kitchen door of the Morse house, and both the door and the latch were deeply textured by exposure to the weather for a century and a half, but the prizes were inside. A relatively simple mantel was ornamented with the portraits of two deceased ancestors, one at each end of the mantel and embedded in it. Sadly, in those days I had avoided photography as a hobby and was not really familiar with historic processes, as I am today. The photos were probably tintypes, but they could have been ambrotypes. In the attic came another architecturally fascinating surprise. An otherwise conventional chimney emerged from the attic floor and then executed a graceful ninety-degree spiral into the roof ridge to emerge on the outside in an orientation parallel to the front of the house. I've never before or since had the privilege of photographing the likes of either detail. It took a day to record the house, and the gracious owners were hospitable to a fault, serving a lunch that would have embarrassed a southern plantation owner.

HABS (and HAER) photography usually follows the work of a summer student team composed of one to seven architectural or engineering students working for about two and one-half months somewhere in America recording from one to a dozen and a half structures through measured drawings, written architectural and historical descriptions, and chains of title. When a number of structures make up a project, they are generally within a thirty-mile radius, more or less.

This is advantageous for the photographer. If the weather is clear when I arrive at a site, I begin shooting exteriors, returning to houses as many times as is necessary to get the light right on the main facade. The photographic

request forms that our teams complete in advance were designed by me to provide essential information, including the name and phone number of the property owner and the direction in which the main facade faces. It is not usually necessary to return to have the light "right" when I know the structure's orientation in advance.

If the weather is overcast when I arrive, I begin by shooting interiors, starting with natural light for illumination and exposing for the light from the windows while providing sufficient artificial light elsewhere to balance the window light. This avoids window burnout.

Since a project of twelve or fifteen structures will easily take a week, clustering the structures, or working from a hub, makes it possible for me to take this approach to dealing with the impact of weather and the light on my work.

A recent project in 1986 to record some sixty structures across Missouri in cooperation with the State Office of Historic Preservation illustrates the success of this plan. The sixty structures were broken down into five clusters strung across the state from East to West. More than five hundred large-format photographs resulted from the intensive thirty-day field assignment.

Sizing up a structure to be documented is my ultimate responsibility. I must work under reasonable time constraints based in part on budget limitations. HABS/HAER documents a structure because of its architectural or engineering merit; historic significance in the accepted sense (Washington slept here) is secondary. A structure by a distinguished architect such as Sullivan, Richardson, or Wright will get more attention than one by Joe Doe.

While working on a structure and becoming more familiar with it, I'll see details worth recording that were not apparent at first. I photograph details in a manner to fill the 5 x 7 plate. This captures texture and particulars revealing craftsmanship as well as design. Throughout an assignment, I try to show the architect's intentions, enthusiasms, and achievements in my photographs as well as the workmanship of the artisans.

In photographing a historic structure, there is always the question of what to exclude or include. The subject can be argued endlessly and justified either way. Generally, my policy is to include everything that is a part of the structure and eliminate anything that is not. In other words, I'll include additions and changes to a structure, even detailing them. I'll exclude people, vehicles, utility poles, trashcans, and even clean up the foreground of debris. There are thousands of my photographs in which pedestrians or vehicles have moved just a millimeter or two out of the camera's range, behind a tree or a column. In other cases, I have moved the camera as little as—literally—a centimeter or two so as not to hide a roof detail behind a tree limb. This precise attention to camera positioning and composition is so important that, after the camera tripod is positioned to the very centimeter, the horizontal and vertical shifts of the view camera's back are then adjusted to the final millimeter.

In the case of the David Ogden house in Fairfield, Connecticut (see photographs 1–3), Bill Lebovich, the architectural historian who provided the captions for the photographs in this book, observes that my photographs make "the viewer sense that this house really is more than two hundred and fifty years old." If I had included a couple more inches in the composition it would have shown a modern lock, destroying the feeling of the two-hundred-year-old door and knocker.

Less tangible a factor to the quality of the finished photograph is the attitude of the owners or occupants to a house. A completely psychological element, attitude has an effect that is inescapable, no matter how dedicated one is to producing a fine photographic record. John and Ann Windle, own-

ers of the extravagant "Shrewsbury" house in Madison, Indiana (see photographs 4–5), were deeply involved in history and preservation. They were proud of their house and that HABS was recording it. Warm and hospitable to a fault, they made me feel both welcome and completely at ease. I could work unhurried. I was pleased with the results. Fortunately, this is the usual reception that greets me, but on occasion . . .

Fate can also play an unexpected hand in a photograph. A picture I made of the entrance to the nave of the beautiful and historic Church of San Jose de Gracia in Trampas, New Mexico (see photographs 18–21), is an excellent example. The photograph was made from the nave, looking out to the gate and courtyard beyond, and the interior door surround is pitch black, with a trace of texture in the rough floor boards visible. This was a nice enough composition, but it was made extraordinary by pure happenstance. At the very moment I tripped the shutter, an ancient New Mexican woman in flawlessly appropriate garb poked her head into the doorway in a cautious, curious manner. I could not have stopped the shutter even had my reflexes permitted or had I wanted to. The result, no credit to me, is one of the photos that I enjoy the most. And the woman's presence enhances the photo as a document.

My quarter-century as a photographer for HABS, which includes some nine years of photographing for HAER, has taken me to every state but Alaska, to Puerto Rico, and to the three American Virgin Islands. I estimate I've made some fifty-five thousand photographs for HABS of, as noted, well over six thousand structures.

In addition, eight of my eleven trips to Europe (not at government expense) have involved photographic assignments and projects, a number of which have been published. These journeys have included Italy, Yugoslavia, France, Hungary, England, Belgium, Holland, Russia, both East and West Germany, Czechoslovakia, and other countries.

In Most, Czechoslovakia during the spring of 1975, the government was in the final throes of a four-year process of preparing to move an entire eleventh-century cathedral in one piece for a distance of a mile or so. James Marston Fitch, historian, academic, and preservationist, and I, following an ICOMOS General Assembly in Rothenberg ob der Tauber, West Germany, were traveling via rented car for two weeks behind the Iron Curtain to visit and study preservation efforts in Berlin, Dresden, and Prague. We learned of the project in Most, and visited there en route to Prague.

We had a letter of introduction to the director of the Most project from the East Germans, and although he was not present when we arrived, we were made most welcome. The cathedral was surrounded by a tall fence, marked with visual signs indicating "no photography!" But inside the fence I had carte blanche to take all the photographs I wanted. And I did, climbing scaffolding to the ceiling and roof in the process.

When finally we left and were driving away, I realized that in order to complete my photo story I needed to photograph the cathedral from a distance to show from whence it was coming and to where it would be moved. But I forgot the "no photography" signs on the fence, and we were now well outside the fence. The inevitable happened. A local citizen, a patriotic octogenarian, I'd judge, was protesting my taking pictures (neither of us could speak the other's language) just as a Czech police car came down the street. I could not communicate with the policemen either, and they gestured me an "invitation" to ride with them in their automobile—a pleasure I'd have been delighted to decline.

Six blocks distant and we were in the police station. Communication was still a prob-

lem, but it was not hard to deduce that "pizpert" meant "passport," and I turned mine over. Since the passport only had about five years or so left to expiration, I was fairly sure it would no longer be valid when next I saw it. I also gave them the letter of introduction, which I fortunately still had in my possession. A very long half-hour passed during which the policemen emerged to look at me once. Then one officer came into the room, his drab khaki uniform with red patches on his collar looking quite official and ominous. But instead of bringing out the cuffs, he handed me my "pizpert" and, with what I presume was a polite smile, said, "you can liff." I think he meant "leave," not "live." But I did both.

Walking back to where I had left the rented car and, incidentally, Professor Fitch, I looked in vain for both. He had not been aware of any of what had transpired. Ten minutes later, while pondering this new development, I saw the car coming toward me, with Fitch at the wheel. He picked me up. "Jack," he said as I settled into my seat, "you should really tell me when you are going to be away for more than a few moments to take pictures. I was concerned, you can get into trouble in these countries!"

I've worked with National Park rangers and naturalists, with architects, engineers, historians, and preservationists, and it is and has been these associations that have made my humble effort to record America's architectural heritage a pleasure and a passion. But whatever I have achieved would never have been possible were it not for the extraordinary people who have composed the staff of the Historic American Buildings Survey and the Historic American Engineering Record over the years.

During an assignment to record Glenmont and the Edison Laboratories in West Orange, New Jersey, many years ago, I was having lunch in what then was the company cafeteria. A tall, elderly gentleman sat down beside me and struck up a conversation. After discussing conservation, preservation, and the Park Service at length, he started asking questions about HABS. Finally, in parting, he said to me, "Young man, you certainly have a fascinating job, and one that will mean much to generations to come!"

We only then exchanged names in full. I shall not forget these parting words from Charles Edison, former governor of New Jersey, secretary of the navy under Franklin D. Roosevelt, and son of Thomas Alva Edison.

DAVID OGDEN HOUSE

Fairfield, Fairfield County, Connecticut
Architect: none
Completed: circa 1720
HABS No. CT-56, photographed 1968

In its simplicity, the Ogden house demonstrates the two major traits of seventeenth- and early eighteenth-century New England residences. First, the architectural tastes of the American Colonists were conservative; they were building in medieval styles that were already more than one hundred years out of vogue in England. Second, in terms of shape and decoration, New England's earliest residences were straightforward, reflecting the limited skills and resources of the colonists and the fact that their concern with being sheltered was more immediate than

any aesthetic considerations.

In his photographs of the door knocker and the shingle siding, Jack Boucher makes the viewer sense that this house really is more than two hundred and fifty years old. The texture of the materials comes right through the photographs. Boucher was not simply producing photographic documentation of an eighteenth-century house, he was transporting the viewer back to the early eighteenth century.

1. West (main) elevation, main entrance, door knocker.
2. North elevation, shingle siding, looking skyward.
3. West (main) and south (side) elevations.

3

CHARLES L. SHREWSBURY HOUSE

Madison, Jefferson County, Indiana
Architect: attributed to Francis Costigan
Completed: 1846
HABS No. IN-8, photographed 1971

Built toward the end of the Greek Revival period (approximately 1820 to 1860), the Shrewsbury house has the pilasters, columned porch, sidelights, cornice, lintels, and other details typical of that style. Yet the delicate, soaring quality of the staircase is more akin to the Federal Style (approximately 1780 to 1820). Both styles drew their inspiration from Classical Greece and Rome, but the Federal interpretation was once characterized as "effeminate," while the Greek Revival has been characterized as "masculine" or robust.

Boucher photographed the exquisite staircase of Shrewsbury house both in color and in black and white. The black-and-white photograph is a fine expression of the structural beauty of the staircase, while the color photograph adds the beauty of the furnishings. Photograph 4 shows the attention to detail (as seen in the ceiling molding) and the tension and movement (of the staircase) that are the hallmarks of outstanding architecture.

4. Center hall with free-standing, spiral stairs.
5. South (rear) elevation.

GEORGE W. BOURNE HOUSE (WEDDING CAKE HOUSE)

Kennebunk, York County, Maine
Architect: unknown
Completed: 1826; gothic ornament applied:
1855
HABS No. ME-74, photographed 1964

Sometimes people forget or do not want to admit that architecture is like clothing in that both are subject to fads. Sometimes an architectural style loses popularity because people have become tired of it; nothing more sophisticated is needed to explain why George Bourne took his chaste late Federal period house and made it into a Gothic artifice. It is interesting to note that the massive Gothic filigree was applied without obstructing the Palladian window in the center bay of the second floor. In fact, the filigree actually repeats and enhances the shape of the Palladian window.

The nineteenth century was marked by a number of architectural styles. The Federal, Classical, and Shingle styles were all more popular for residences than the Gothic Style. Perhaps the Gothic has been so closely associated with institutional architecture—churches and colleges—that people considered it inappropriate for their homes.

Photograph 6, of the pinnacle, demonstrates one of Boucher's basic principles of architectural photography: pick an angle that will draw the viewer's eye into the photograph.

6. Southeast corner, details of the pinnacle, cornice, and balustrade.
7. South (main) elevation.

TIMOTHY BROWN HOUSE (BROWN'S TEMPLE, SPIRIT HOUSE)

Georgetown, Madison County, New York
Architect: none
Completed: circa 1865
HABS No. NY-5602, photographed 1966

Brown believed that spirits lived in the closets of his house and directed him to decorate the house as it now appears.

One never sees the Timothy Brown house in American architectural histories because such individualistic statements are impossible to fit into the usual stylistic summaries of architecture. Yet Brown's work is part of the American tradition of handcrafting buildings (primarily residences) without the involvement of architects.

8. West (main) elevation.

9. Northwest corner, elaborately ornamented cornice.

10. Northwest corner, detail of carved column.

I. N. HAGAN HOUSE

Chalkhill, Fayette County, Pennsylvania
Architect: Frank Lloyd Wright
Completed: 1954
HABS No. PA-5347, photographed 1985

Jack Boucher can be immensely charming and personable. One of the benefits of this aspect of his personality is that people never see him as a photographer who should be left alone and only checked on occasionally to make sure he has not knocked anything over with his tripod. When Boucher was photographing Frank Lloyd Wright's Fallingwater (see photographs 40–49), the curator there told him about the Hagan house, and Boucher went over to look at it. He was sufficiently impressed with this late example of Wright's domestic architecture to ask for per-

mission to photograph it. If anyone else had been sent to photograph Fallingwater, the HABS collection would not have also gained photographs of the Hagan house, which was built by friends of the Kaufmanns and admirers of Fallingwater. Shortly after Boucher photographed it, the Hagan house was sold and nearly destroyed by fire. Boucher's photographs became an important source for restoration work.

Although vastly different in appearance, the Hagan house has strong similarities with Wright's much earlier Prairie Style houses. In the latter, as in the Hagan house, Wright wanted to integrate the house with the ground, suggesting powerful horizontal massing. And, in both, small detailing relieves large exterior planes.

12

13

11. Battered stone wall and cantilevered roof.

12. Eave with skylights.

13. Wright's signature block on the west elevation. This block was in the same color as Wright's Cadillac, Cherokee red, his favorite color.

44

WILLIAM M. CARSON HOUSE (INGOMAR CLUB)

Eureka, Humboldt County, California
Architect: Newsom Brothers

Completed: 1886
HABS No. CA-1911, photographed 1960

With its asymmetry and elaborate surface treatments, both exterior and interior, the Carson house most closely fits into the Queen Anne Style. But to pigeonhole this house into any stylistic classification is to deny both its uniqueness and the uniqueness of the design tastes of Samuel Newsom (1854–1908) and Joseph Cathen Newsom (1858–1930). The Newsoms, who learned architecture by apprenticing in their older brother's office, were successful and prodigious, designing more than six hundred buildings in California as well as having commissions that ranged from the Orient to Europe.

Because of its exuberance, the Carson house is one of the best known and most photographed houses in American architectural history. Despite the frequency with which it has been photographed, the Carson house as captured by Boucher (especially the porch view, photograph 15) does look fresh and different.

14. West (main) elevation.
15. View of the porch, looking south.
16. Second floor hall, looking east.
17. Second floor hall, detail of the base of an arch.

14

SAN JOSE DE GRACIA CHURCH

Trampas, Taos County, New Mexico
Architect: unknown
Completed: circa 1770
HABS No. NM-61, photographed 1961

Several of the churches built by the Spanish missionaries are better known than San Jose de Gracia, but none better expresses the merging of Spanish Roman Catholicism and American Indian spiritualism.

San Jose de Gracia Church is more modest yet typical of the churches and governmental buildings erected by the Spaniards in their colonies. Even the churches with towers read as horizontal structures with largely flat surfaces. The small intricate detailing seen in the larger, more ornate Spanish churches has

impact because it contrasts with the planar surfaces.

18. Nave (west end), painted ceiling.

19. Nave, looking east toward chancel. Note the tripod and camera of the late Bainbridge Bunting—the prominent architectural historian who was accompanying Boucher—which were inadvertently left in the photograph.

20. Nave, looking west toward entrance and gate beyond. This image, with the Indian woman looking in to see what Boucher is doing, is one of his favorites and one of his few with people.

21. West (main) elevation and gate.

22

CHURCH OF THE HOLY CROSS

Stateburg, Sumter County, South Carolina
Architect: Edward C. Jones
Completed: 1852
HABS No. SC-13-14, photographed 1985

Constructed of rammed earth, the Church of the Holy Cross is a powerful yet dignified articulation of the Gothic Revival, and Boucher quite admirably captured these qualities. The Gothic Revival in the United States has always enjoyed its greatest popularity for church designs. In fact, even some Jewish groups (usually Reformed) have erected Gothic synagogues. Residences with Gothic detailing are as visually compelling as Gothic religious structures, but much less common. The Church of the Holy Cross demonstrates that the Gothic Style is as effective in a rural church as it is in an urban one.

Photograph 22, of the grave marker, is so dramatic because of the shadow, which was cast by Boucher's hand-held flash. He used the flash not to create that effect but to assure that the lettering on the stone would be legible.

22. Grave marker of the Adams family, abutting the foundation at the northeast corner of the north transept. Note that the church was built after John Coit and Charles Adams were buried. It is not known whether building the church virtually on top of them was a way of honoring or of damning their memory.

23. North elevation.

23

56

DUNMORE METHODIST CHURCH

Dunmore, Pocahontas County, West Virginia
Architect: if any, unknown
Completed: 1891
HABS No. WV-54, photographed 1963

With its emphasis on surface decoration and suggestion of structural members, Dunmore Methodist Church belongs to the Stick Style most popular in the 1870s. The Stick Style remained popular into the 1890s in more iso-

lated areas such as West Virginia and California.

In its simplicity, the Dunmore Methodist Church is utterly compelling. A good photographer knows when not to get in the way of a strong subject.

24. East (main) elevation.
25. East (main) elevation, detail.

24

HEALY BUILDING, GEORGETOWN UNIVERSITY

Washington, D.C.
Architect: Smithmeyer & Pelz
Completed: 1879
HABS No. DC-248, photographed 1969

Healy Building sits atop a hill in George-town, overlooking the Potomac River. Designed in a style suggestive of Richardsonian Romanesque and Austrian Gothic municipal architecture, the building has an elongated clock tower that further exaggerates its prominent location. Smithmeyer & Pelz are best known as the architects of the Library of Congress building.

It is not surprising that the Healy Building has a certain Austrian flavor, since John L. Smithmeyer (1832–1908) was born in Austria and Paul Johannes Pelz (1841–1918), who

was the chief designer in the firm, was born and educated in Prussia. Pelz also traveled in Europe in 1873, refreshing and expanding his knowledge of European architectural antecedents.

26. East (main) elevation. In the foreground is a statue of the Reverend John Carroll, who founded Georgetown University in 1789. Healy Building is named after the Reverend Patrick Healy, president of the university from 1874 to 1882.

27. East (main) elevation, at intersection of main pavilion and projecting, north pavilion. This illustration is an excellent example of how much information Boucher can pack into a photograph while retaining a strong, compelling image.

CHESHIRE MILL, NUMBER ONE

Harrisville, Cheshire County, New Hampshire
Architect: Cyrus Harris

Completed: 1847
HABS No. NH-173, photographed 1969

Harrisville was a town founded in the early to mid-nineteenth century by the Harris family. The site was picked because of the natural water supply, which could be used to power the textile machines, and the buildings were built of local stone and locally made bricks.

The granite-and-brick mill buildings are typical of early New England industrial communities. Although these buildings are utilitarian, the combination of contrasting colors, fine proportions, and carefully chiseled details such as the lintels and cornice produces buildings of enduring attractiveness.

Boucher has captured, especially in photograph 29, the dignity and beauty possible when local materials are built into simple, familiar forms, with limited concern for ornamentation.

28. West (main) elevation, flanked by later mill buildings.
29. West (main) elevation, detail view showing cornice return and portion of decorative cast-iron fire stair.

28

30

TEXAS STATE CAPITOL

Austin, Travis County, Texas
Architect: Elijah E. Myers (1832-1909)
Completed: 1888
HABS No. TX-3326, photographed 1966

Myers was a prolific and extremely contro-
versial designer of government buildings. His
unsuccessful opponents accused him of win-
ning design competitions through bribery,
and he was frequently investigated for extended delays and cost overruns.

From the early 1870s to the early 1890s,
roughly the period of the Richardsonian Romanesque, American architecture achieved a
vigor, monumentality, and power to uplift the
viewer that has never been matched. The
rough-hewed facing and the solidity of the
massing of Myers's Texas State Capitol or H.
H. Richardson's Trinity Church (1872-1877),
Boston, Massachusetts, are utterly compelling like few other buildings in the United
States.

30. Rotunda, partial view of second-floor
gallery.
31. Ceiling of dome.
32. West hall, first floor.
33. South (main) elevation, with the
Heroes of the Alamo monument in the
foreground. The Goddess of Liberty stands
atop the building's dome.

STRATFORD HALL

Stratford, Westmoreland County, Virginia
Architect: unknown
Completed: circa 1730
HABS No. VA-307, photographed 1969

Stratford Hall is the home of the Lee family, known for its involvement in the founding of this country and for Robert E. Lee's role in the Civil War. It was restored by Dr. Fiske Kimball in the 1930s, and some of his treatments appear to be based more on his tastes than on physical evidence.

The theater critic Brendan Gill once said he divided buildings into two groups—those that sit and those that stand. Stratford Hall definitely falls into the former group. That is not to say that it is intimidated or over-whelmed by the earth, but rather that it has equal footing with, and sits firmly on, the ground. Stratford Hall is a proud, three-dimensional structure and an appropriate ancestral home for the Lees.

Photograph 34 is one of Boucher's strongest images. It has a strong focus in the far chimney, and the entire frame is filled—top, bottom, and sides—by the near chimney.

34. View from balcony of the west group of chimneys, looking toward the east group of chimneys. From a documentary standpoint, the framing clearly shows the existence of a twin chimney.

35. South (main) elevation.

35

JOSEPH MORSE HOUSE (STONE HOUSE)

Eaton Village, Madison County, New York
Architect: unknown
Completed: 1802; enlarged: 1846
HABS No. NY-5603, photographed 1963

The Morse house is an excellent example of the Greek Revival residences so popular in upstate New York. This house is particularly interesting for its primitive touches such as the door latch and the mantel.

With its massive fluted Ionic columns, large, unadorned entablature (the band above the columns' capitals), gable end, and stone walls, the Morse house has a robustness especially appropriate to Greek (and Classical) Revival houses.

36. East (main) elevation, with kitchen wing.
37. Iron latch on kitchen door.
38. Northeast room, first floor, fireplace mantel decorated with naive artwork, including two images of deceased family members.
39. Attic. The chimney is twisted so that the part above the roofline will be parallel to the front elevation.

38

FALLINGWATER (KAUFMANN HOUSE)

Bear Run, Fayette County, Pennsylvania
Architect: Frank Lloyd Wright
Completed: 1939
HABS No. PA-5346, photographed 1985

Frank Lloyd Wright (1869–1959) is probably best known for his inventive Prairie Style houses or his idiosyncratic buildings such as the Guggenheim Museum. But he was influenced by other architects and architecture such as the Japanese (an influence he denied). Fallingwater is clearly influenced by International Style or Modern (a better term) architects such as Le Corbusier. But, at Fallingwater, Wright took the best of Le Corbusier—his gutsy expression of architecture—made it even stronger, and incorporated it with nature.

When Boucher is asked to name his favorite period of American architecture to photograph, he routinely replies that he has no favorite because otherwise he would not be able objectively to photograph all periods. In reality, Boucher's favorite is probably the nineteenth century, and, therefore, he was not overwhelmed with the assignment to photograph Wright's brilliantly personal interpretation of the International Style, Fallingwater. At least, he was not until he arrived at the house, when one of the first things he did was call back to the office to share his excitement at the prospect of photographing the building and its environment.

40. East and south elevations as seen from the approach bridge, looking northwest.
41. Living room, looking southeast, showing the trellis skylight.

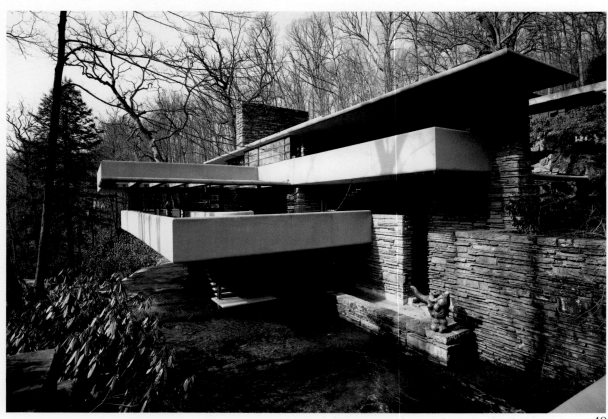

40

42. Steps from the living room to the stream below. Boucher photographed the steps with the hatch cover open (as shown here) and with the hatch cover closed. This concern with providing comprehensive photographic documentation of even the smallest detail is typical of Boucher.

43. View from inside the guest house looking east toward the patio and pool.

44. Bottom portion of the stairway from the living room to the stream, with a partial view of the cantilevered terrace leading to the living room.

45. Corner of second-floor bedroom, on west side of house.

46. The view from the landing on third floor looking east.

47. The steps leading down the hill from the guest house to the main house, looking south. Note the expressive stepped thin concrete canopy.

48. The view from the house looking north toward the guest house.

49. View from downstream looking northeast.

SHAKER CHURCH FAMILY ROUND BARN

Hancock, Berkshire County, Massachusetts
Architect: none
Completed: 1826
HABS No. MA-674, photographed 1962

The round barn shows that in the hands of sensitive people such as the Shakers even the most utilitarian of buildings can be works of quiet beauty. For most cultures, the only building that is intended to make a religious statement is the church. The Shakers ex-pressed their religion in every building and every object they created.

Boucher photographed the roof trusses both as vertical (not shown) and as horizontal images, each one capturing different details and making different statements. This type of comprehensive coverage is characteristic of Boucher and the Historic American Buildings Survey.

50. Roof trusses for the circular monitor and the lantern above it.
51. North (main) elevation, detail showing date stone and major openings.
52. North (main) elevation.

52

NICHOLS-WANTON-HUNTER HOUSE

Newport, Newport County, Rhode Island
Architect: unknown
Completed: circa 1750
HABS No. RI-7, photographed 1971

With the mid-eighteenth century, the American colonists started building houses, churches, and government buildings that displayed a concern for style and decoration. This Georgian architecture marked the end of the colonists' concentration by and large on merely sheltering themselves and the beginning of a new desire to create architecture that addressed their artistic as well as their physical needs. Newport was an important eighteenth-century furniture-making city, and the skill of its craftsmen is reflected in the woodwork in this house.

Boucher once said that he likes to bring the camera in as close as it will focus when he photographs details. That approach can be seen in the way he isolated the cherub on the china cupboard in photograph 55. Naturally, Boucher also shot more general views showing the cherub as part of the entire cupboard and as part of the entire room.

53. Central hall, looking west.
54. Central hall, detail of stair balustrade. Each of the three balusters on the tread has a different turning.
55. Parlor, carved cherub on china cupboard.

55

56

MILFORD (GOVERNOR JOHN LAWRENCE MANNING PLANTATION)

Pinewood Vicinity, Sumter County,
     South Carolina
Architect: "Mr. Potter"
Completed: circa 1850
HABS No. SC-257, photographed 1960

In rural upstate New York, Ohio, New England, and the South it is possible to identify the towns that were settled in the early nineteenth century by their Roman and Grecian place names. The interest in anything classical extended to children's names, clothing, furniture, and architecture. Perhaps reacting to the commonplace Classical architecture, a mid-nineteenth-century American architectural critic wrote that it was boring and, furthermore, dishonest that every type of building looked like a Grecian temple. From

the vantage point of the late twentieth century, we can say that the architectural landscape is considerably richer because of Grecian temples like Milford.

These four images show Boucher's flexibility as a photographer. Each shot succeeds as photographic documentation, yet each also manages to convey the mood of the house. And the photographs range from a detail shot to a telephoto shot to an interior shot to one of an oblique exterior.

56. Portico, detail showing entablature and capital.
57. Portico, looking west.
58. Entrance hall, hot-air register.
59. Entrance hall, looking toward staircase in rear.

SAMUEL GILBERT HATHAWAY HOUSE (HATHAWAY HALL)

Solon, Cortland County, New York
Architect: unknown

Completed: 1866
HABS No. NY-5592, photographed 1966

Hathaway built his house in 1844–1845 but doubled its size in 1866, creating this substantial if unexciting Classical Revival residence. Hathaway was one of those multi-talented nineteenth-century gentlemen, having served as a major general, a state senator, and a U.S. congressman, all before he built this house.

The Ionic-columned porch and wide cornice place this house in the Greek Revival Style, although the quoins (large blocks at the corners) and roof balustrade suggest that the owner was not locked into a style but willing to mix elements to create a picturesque elevation.

60. Attic with small dormers and stairs to roof. This image demonstrates Boucher's ability to use artificial lighting to effectively and evenly illuminate an area that would otherwise have substantial light and dark contrasts. Without Boucher's deft touch, many of the structural elements would not have been visible in the print.

61. Center hall, newel post and stairs with fret motif on string.

62. South (main) elevation. By using the granite gateposts to frame his photograph, Boucher not only created a nice composition but also conveyed how the house would look to someone approaching it.

HENRY M. FLAGLER MANSION (WHITEHALL)

Palm Beach, Palm Beach County, Florida
Architect: Carrère & Hastings
Completed: 1902
HABS No. FL-224, photographed 1972

Henry Flagler was one of the first if not the first to realize the commercial potential of Florida as a winter resort. He built hotels for the tourists and then built trains to make sure the tourists could get to the hotels. As the photographs of his mansion demonstrate, he was amply rewarded for his imagination.

It was Henry Flagler who encouraged John Merven Carrère (1858–1911) and Thomas Hastings (1860–1929) to leave their positions as draftsmen at McKim, Mead & White and open their own firm. Carrère & Hastings went on to design at least two hotels and churches for Flagler. Carrère and Hastings were both educated at the École des Beaux Arts, and their designs exemplified the French emphasis on symmetry, monumentality, and axial organization as seen in such important buildings as the New York Public Library (1902–1911).

63. East (main) elevation.
64. Grand hall, ceiling detail.
65. Grand hall.

64

65

GUNSTON HALL

Lorton, Fairfax County, Virginia
Architect: William Buckland
Completed: circa 1750
HABS No. VA-141, photographed 1981

Gunston Hall was built for George Mason, an important if underappreciated Revolutionary War statesman. However, Gunston Hall is known primarily for its magnificent wood

carving done by William Buckland, who was trained in London and came to the colonies as an indentured servant.

The two most notable features of Gunston Hall are how dissimilar the exterior and interior are and how closely related the house is to its setting. Traditionally, the main elevation of a house suggests the interior plan and decoration. But the largely plain, low exterior of Gunston Hall barely hints at the center-stair plan and virtually denies the extremely sophisticated level of surface treatment in the rooms. The front entrance of Gunston Hall is on line with a magnificent enfilade of trees. The back entrance opens onto a formal English garden from which the land falls off toward a distant river.

66. Approach to north (main) elevation, flanked by rows of trees.
67. Palladian Room, detail of door surround.
68. Palladian Room, partial view of elaborate carved door surround and door panel.
69. Palladian Room, detail of cornice.
70. West elevation. Note how the shadow emphasizes the three-dimensional quality of the eave and the projecting basement entrance. The shadow also adds a strong graphic element.

66

68

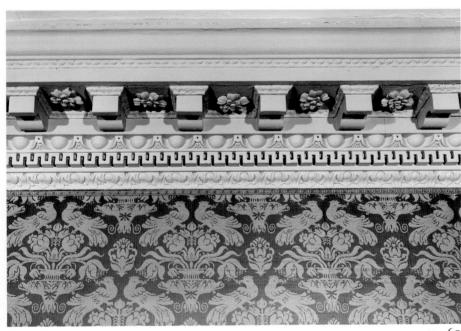

69

71

JOHNSON WAX CORPORATION BUILDING

Racine, Racine County, Wisconsin
Architect: Frank Lloyd Wright
Completed: 1947
HABS No. WI-284, photographed 1969

The building was completed in the late 1930s, but the tower was added nearly ten years later. Both share strong curvilinear shapes.

Johnson Wax is a much better building—more unified, simpler—than some of Wright's more widely known projects such as the Guggenheim Museum. Often Wright's strong structural statements are compromised by dated, inappropriate decoration or a clash of shapes. The Johnson Wax building suffers none of these problems. The tower is especially interesting because Wright suspended

the floors out from the central core and used glass tubing as a surface material.

71. Reception lobby, looking west.

72. Bridge over the parking area, looking north. The half-round top of the bridge consists of bands of glass tubes.

73. South side of the tower. A photograph with converging verticals is not typical of either Jack Boucher or the Historic American Buildings Survey, but Boucher felt the size and location of the tower justified the convergence. He feels there are exceptions to rules, even his conviction that perspective correction is essential to documentary architectural photography.

74. Reception lobby, partial view of a corner of the glass wall enclosing the space.